To Ian

AURICULAS

An essential guide

AURICULAS
An essential guide

Paul Dorey

THE CROWOOD PRESS

First published in 2011 by
The Crowood Press Ltd
Ramsbury, Marlborough
Wiltshire SN8 2HR

www.crowood.com

British Library Cataloguing-in-Publication Data
A catalogue record for this book is available from the British Library.

ISBN 978 1 84797 286 6

Front cover:
Photographs by the author, except bottom two, courtesy of Drointon
Nurseries of Plaster Pitts, Norton Conyers, Ripon, North Yorkshire

All photographs are by the author unless otherwise specified.

Acknowledgements
I would like to thank the proprietors of Drointon Nurseries, Norton
Conyers, Ripon, North Yorkshire, and Gabriel Ash, Superior Greenhouses
of Farndon, Near Chester for the use of their photographs. My thanks to
Kath Harris for her understanding, indulgence and support. Finally, and
not least, thanks are given to Matthew Dorey for his technical expertise
in compiling this book. His invaluable contribution and his great patience
have made it possible.

Typeset by Servis Filmsetting Ltd, Stockport, Cheshire
Printed and bound in Malaysia by Times Offset (M) Sdn Bhd

Contents

1 The History of the Auricula

Historically auriculas are quite remarkable and have a significant place in ornamental horticulture. They have been cultivated in Great Britain since the middle of the sixteenth century and became one of the eight classic florists' flowers. Auriculas were originally imported from the high Alps of Europe and such was the demand for some of the cultivated varieties that some select ones changed hands for prices as high as £20 each during the seventeenth century. When one considers that a merchant's wage was, in those times, around £100 per annum and a parson (quite a few of the clergy were keen flower growers) would receive around £20 per year, then it is clear that only the lucky few were able to collect the most prized of auricula cultivars.

With their extraordinary combined charms of delicate scent and vivid colours, the auriculas as we know them today are quite different from their ancestors. Sometimes referred to as 'Living Antiques', they are cultivated hardy flowering alpine plants developed over centuries by skilled florists dedicated to cultivating flowers of perfection.

The auricula story begins not on these shores, but in the European Alps of France

OPPOSITE PAGE:
Auriculas in the greenhouse.

Today's auricula has been developed over centuries.

(the Jura and the Vosges), the mountainous regions of the Black Forest of Germany and the Tatra mountains between Poland and Slovakia.

Research shows that the forebears of the modern day auricula were the *Primula auricula,* once known as *Primula ursi,* which is a small yellow flowering alpine plant of the Alps, and *Primula hirsuta* syn. *rubra* of mauve to pink flowers. The natural cross produced *Primula pubescens (auricula ursi II)* and it is believed that it is the descendants of this cross that have been in cultivation now for a period of more than 400 years. Dioscrides talked about them in AD50 and called them *Sanicula alpina.*

The exact parentage of the modern-day auriculas is shrouded in mystery; some eminent florists, or to use the more modern term, auricula growers, believe that all of the modern-day auriculas should be recognized as *P. pubescens* and not *P. auricula.* The debate still goes on but the important point is that we continue to grow and develop new cultivars whatever the auriculas' lineage.

Identification of the natural auricula shows a rosette form of alpine plant growing at an altitude of at least 1,000m and up to 1,900m; it thrives in limestone grassland and has sweet-scented, salver form (trumpet-shaped) flowers of deep yellow. There is often a ring of farina, a white powdery substance, in the centre of the flower, which adds to the attraction of this simple alpine plant. Some plants have a dusting of farina to varying degrees on their foliage and sometimes also on the scape (flower stalk).

Species of the *Primula* Genus

- There are more than 400 different species of the genus *Primula*.
- The name *Primula* means first in Latin, relating to their early flowering.
- They are mainly native to the northern hemisphere.
- They mostly prefer dappled sunlight and well drained soils.
- Some of most widely grown species of *Primula* are:

P. allionii,	P. elatior,
P. alpicola,	P. florindae,
P. auricula,	P. japonica,
P. beesiana,	P. marginata,
P. bulleyana,	P. pubescens,
P. chungensis,	P. sieboldii,
P. cockburniana,	P. veris
P. denticulata,	P. vulgaris

It was in 1596 that Gaspar Bauhin (1560–1624), professor of botany, anatomy and medicine at the University of Basel, Switzerland named twelve sorts of auricula. In Vienna, Clusius (Charles de L'écluse, 1526–1609), was a noted botanist and traveller, who was born in Arras, Flanders (now France). He became a doctor and, later on, an avid plant expeditionist. During the period 1550–75

he undertook expeditions throughout continental Europe and discovered different species of narcissi and iris in Spain and Portugal and *P. auricula* in Hungary and Austria. He sent auricula plants to John Gerard (1545–1612) back in England for garden cultivation.

Clusius was famous during his time for gathering new plants from around the Middle East and Europe, growing them on and sending plant material, including the tulip, to other enthusiasts. Clusius became *horti praefectus* (head gardener and curator) at Leiden University and was charged with the development of a new botanic garden there. In 1601 Clusius wrote his tome *Opera Omnia Rariorum Plantarum Historia*. He described six types of auriculas that he grew for the Emperor Maximillian II (1527–76), the Holy Roman emperor.

During the sixteenth century English botanist John Gerard, who became superintendent of the gardens of William Cecil, advisor to Queen Elizabeth, also becoming Master of the Company of Barber Surgeons, referred to auriculas in his publication *Herball, or Generall Historie of Plantes* (1597) as 'Beares ears'. He was also known to refer to them as 'Mountain Cowslips'. It can be learnt from his drawings and narrative that there were auriculas of seven differing colours including yellow, purple, scarlet, blush and red shades under cultivation at this time. Gerard describes in his tome that there were:

- Auricula *vr fiflore luteo*, Yellow Beares-eare
- Auricula *vr fiflore purpureo*, Purple Beares-eare
- Auricula *vr fi ljclufij*, Red Beares-eare
- Auricula *vr fiiy clufy*, Scarlet Beares-eare
- Auricula *vr fierukefcens*, Blufh [blush] coloured Beares-eare
- Auricula *vr fi fuane rubens*, Bright red Beares-eare and
- Auricula *vr fi minima stamell*, Beares eare [stamell is a red colour].

History shows that Innsbruck, the capital of the Austrian region of the Tyrol, was an area of the Alps where auriculas were growing high up in the mountain ranges. It was from here that some plant hunters and other prominent people dug up auriculas to transplant back to their protected gardens where they were grown for their beauty. The auricula was also noted as a plant with medicinal properties, extracts of which were used to treat palsies, cramps and convulsions, making the plant even more of an attraction. As described by Gerard, '[...]the Swiss called them "Schwindlekraut" and used the rootes for strengthening of the head, so when they are on top of places that are high "giddiness" and swimming of the "braine" may not affect them'.[1]

From these mountainous European regions auriculas were transported across the continent to various parts. They eventually reached all areas of Great Britain, at the latest in 1629, as far as can be gathered from Thomas Johnson's *Iter Plantarum* at Magdalen College, Oxford. In this work Johnson (*c*.1600–44) describes 'a great many varieties' (of auriculas) growing in the Lambeth, London garden of Mr John Tradescant (1608–62), Gardener Royal to Charles I. Tradescant was an avid plantsman and florist who, through careful selection and breeding, improved the auricula and exported new cultivars back to his native Holland as well as importing others. It is thought that it was these plant exchanges that brought the auricula into the consciousness of noted herbalists, florists and keen gardeners in England, rather than the theory of escaping Flemish weavers bringing auriculas with them as they fled their country to escape persecution. However, we are not certain; perhaps it was a combination of both these activities.

Tradescant had inherited a garden, and also a museum known as the 'Ark', from his father John Tradescant the Elder (1570–1638). After the death of his father, Tradescant the Younger succeeded as 'Keeper of the Gardens, Vines and Silkworms' at the long-demolished Oatlands Palace in Weybridge, Surrey. The Tradescants contributed a great deal to English horticulture and their name lives on today.

John Parkinson (1566–1650), in his *Paradisi in Sole Paradisus Terrestris* published in 1629, says that some growers were sowing so many auriculas that there were too many to count

The auricula originally grew in the high Alps of Europe.

them all. He described twenty-one cultivars, many of which had been improved in size by florists. Gerard had said that auricula pips were on the small side, but according to Parkinson and others they knew of larger pips of between eight and thirteen in number in a truss as a result of florists' breeding.

Parkinson described two distinct groups of auriculas in which some had a white eye and the other a gold eye, hence the gold-centred and light-centred auriculas with which we are familiar today. He also differentiated between the foliage as some having 'mealiness' and others as being 'meal-less'. In his *Theatrum Botanicum* (*c*.1640) mention is made of 'variously stript' (striped) auriculas, which is probably the first recorded mention of the striped auriculas.

Parkinson was appointed Apothecary to James I (1566–1625) and after the publication of his *Paradisi in Sole Paradisus Terrestris*, Charles I (1600–49) bestowed on him the title of Botanicus Regius Primarius (Royal Botanist). In his garden at Long Acre, Covent Garden, London, Parkinson had many rarities growing, reputed to be 484 in number. He was well acquainted with both John Gerard and John Tradescant. Parkinson's work, observations and writings are a valuable reference for the auricula history enthusiast and students of theatrical gardening.

Another noted figure of this time is aristocrat Sir Thomas Hanmer, Bart (1612–80). Hanmer, from a distinguished family of Welsh kings, was a page and cup bearer to Charles I; he later became a gardener and garden writer and contributed his important work *The Garden Book*, which was completed in 1659 but not published until 1933. *The Garden Book* is regarded as one of the most important gardening books in the English language and much of the information contained in it was probably gleaned during Hanmer's Civil War exile in France, Holland and Italy. Returning to his ancestral seat Bettisfield Park near Hanmer, Whitchurch in Shropshire (which was then part of Flintshire), Sir Thomas devoted his energies to gardening and the study of plants. Like many keen gardeners of his time, Sir Thomas favoured tulips, and famously introduced Tulipa variety *Agate Hanmer* to England.

Sir Thomas Hanmer, Bart

- Thomas Hanmer was born in 1612.
- He was descended from a line of Welsh kings.
- He was a staunch loyalist.
- He had a very large collection of plants at Bettisfield, Flintshire including many auriculas.
- He was made a cup bearer to Charles I at the tender age of twelve.
- His favourite flower was the tulip but he was also very fond of auriculas, singing their praises in his publication *The Garden Book of Sir Thomas Hanmer.*

Sir Thomas also cultivated anemones, primroses, cowslips and beares ears (auriculas). He grew his auriculas under a north wall at his garden in Bettisfield. He was regarded as a knowledgeable horticulturalist, avid grower and was arguably the leading gardening figure of his era. He described auriculas as a type of sweetly scented cowslip that was easy to propagate from and had beautiful flowers. It was noted by him that auriculas were spring-flowering plants that sometimes flowered again in August or September.

Sir Thomas says that in his time there were auriculas of white, yellow, 'haire colours', orange, and various shades of red, including: cherry, crimson and other red colours, violets and purples. Other colour descriptions that are not familiar to us today include murreys, olives, cinnamon colours, ash colours, leathercoates and dunns. He goes on to say that there were stript or border'd types, which are probably the striped auriculas, and of these there was one with stripes of white and purple, and another, which was scarcer, of purple and yellow. Sir Thomas mentions names given to some auriculas such as the Emperour, the Prince of Wales, Humphreys, Royal Orenge and Prince of Orenge.

Sir Thomas gives us examples of the compost he recommended for potting auriculas, stating that it should not be too rich or, if it is, the compost must not be too moist. The compost in those far-off times was composed of ingredients such as 'good black mold' mixed together with cow manure that had been stood for a while. This mixture was put into boxes and then salt mixed with sand was placed on top of the compost to help keep worms away. It is reasonable to assume that this concoction was also effective in keeping slugs and snails away, but no mention is made of these pests. It is pointed out that auriculas do not prosper out of the shade but do well with the protection of a wall. As modern-day growers know, auriculas do not grow well in full sunshine, but the border and alpine types thrive in a lightly shaded and sheltered spot.

With the winters being much harder and longer in those times the foliage of auriculas would completely die down in the icy and snowy conditions of this season. Frosts did not harm the auriculas as they are very hardy plants, however the carrots (the thick part of the root) tended to pull themselves out of the earth a little during thawing periods but were fine if placed back into the ground immediately. By the end of February fresh top dressing was put over the roots to protect them from the icy March winds.

The division or splitting of auricula roots took place at any time of the year, apart from winter, with towards the end of August being the preferred time for this operation. Ripened seed was generally sown in October but was on some occasions kept over and sown in February, which is the preferred month to sow these days. The compost mixture for sowing auriculas, black mould and well-rotted cow manure, was the same as the mixture for potting but was well sieved. The boxes were filled to around a foot at the rims and then a thin layer of the sand and salt mix was added again as pest protection. Finally, sieved willow earth at least an inch in depth would be placed on the boxes; if willow earth was not available then sifted manure would be used.

Auricula seed was sown quite thickly and a layer of finely sieved compost was used to just cover the seeds to afford protection from birds and the wind. The boxes were left in a shaded spot and covered with mosses for protection from frosts, rain and snow. By late April to May germination would have taken place. The most advanced seedlings would be pricked off to small pots of compost, watered and then placed out of the sun to grow on.

Writing in 1659 Sir Thomas refers to a gentleman by the name of 'Tuggy in Westminster' as the first sower of auricula seed 'of some good ones out of Great Leathercote bearing this name'.[2] John Rea (d. 1681) of Shropshire, writing thirty-two years after Tuggy's death, also refers to this variety. It seems that Ralph Tuggy was an eminent nurseryman/florist of Westminster, London, known also to John Parkinson and Thomas Johnson. It is thought that the bard William Shakespeare also visited Tuggy's garden.

Mary Somerset, née Capel (1630–1715), Duchess of Beaufort and former Lady Beauchamp, was an avid horticulturalist and collector of plants. She married Henry Somerset (1629–1700) who was the third Marquis of Worcester and became the first Duke of Beaufort in 1659. Historical accounts tell us that the couple, shortly after their marriage, set about restoring the country estate of Badminton in Gloucestershire after the Civil Wars that had wreaked havoc throughout the country.

The energy and determination of this remarkable aristocratic couple created a garden paradise at Badminton. In the late 1660s Henry began to landscape the grounds and added ninety acres to his deer park, increasing the size of the estate to 900 acres. The installation of garden features included a maze, avenues of elm and ash trees, an orangery, twelve radial pathways and glasshouses to house many exotic plants brought to these shores from around the globe. The collection is thought to have included specimens in the high hundreds. Mary also collected gardening books penned during her time, and titles such as John Parkinson's *Paradisi in Sole Paradisus Terrestris* and John Gerard's *Herball, or Generall Historie of Plantes* would have been available to her.

Henry Somerset was a prominent political figure. He was a member of the Privy Council of Charles II, and Lord-Lieutenant of Bristol,

Gloucester, Herefordshire and Monmouthshire and was also Lord President of the Welsh Marches. In these important roles he wielded much influence over a large part of the West Country and South Wales. As his business kept him away from his Badminton estate for long periods of time it fell to Mary, an aristocrat by birth, to run the estate, dealing with the administration and accounts. She also found the time to embrace the science of botany and help create the magnificent landscape and gardens at Badminton, and bring up six children.

In 1681 Henry bought a property in Chelsea, London that he named 'Chelsea House', also known as Beaufort House, which was during the sixteenth century the home of Sir Thomas More. The grand house stood in fifteen acres of land and cost him £15,000 to purchase. At first Mary was reluctant to spend time in Chelsea but the couple began to entertain there and so the grounds needed to be improved. Eventually the couple set about landscaping the property in the same style as at Badminton.

Mary amassed a large collection of exotic plants at Chelsea House and Badminton, which became the largest collection in England. She obtained seeds and propagating materials from plants given to her by plant hunters of the day, including physician and botanist Sir Hans Sloane (1660–1753) of science and drinking chocolate fame, for cultivating at both of her properties.

Apart from the exotics being sent from around the globe, Mary Somerset also collected alpine plants including auriculas, of which she grew many in the borders and displayed in auricula theatres. The remarkable Mary Somerset made an invaluable contribution to horticulture. Her dried flower collection in a twelve-volume herbarium is, today, in the protection of the Natural History Museum in London.

John Rea, another eminent gardener, in 1676 published his book *Flora: seu, De Florum Cultura or, A complete Florilege Furnished With all Requisites belonging to a Florist*. In the third edition, c.1702, which was dedicated to Sir Thomas Hanmer and his family, Rea describes many auricula varieties and the raisers of these plants. Rea was a gardener and nurseryman from Kinlet, Shropshire, who was reputed to have the most extensive collection of tulips in England at this time. He undertook the writing of his book as he felt that Parkinson's *Paradisi in Sole Paradisus Terrestris* was not sufficiently up to date as there had been many more plant discoveries since its publication. Rea laid out his work in three sections: 'The Flora', in which he dealt with enclosed garden flowers; 'The Ceres', where he writes on the preferred annuals flowers from seed; and 'The Pomona', which dealt with fruit trees.

On its publication Rea's book was regarded as a seminal work on the cultivation of flowers. Rea also designed the gardens at Gerard's Bromley, Staffordshire, which was the seat of Baron Gerard. John Rea has often been confused with John Ray (1627–1705), who was a naturalist.

Mr William Hughes, horticulture writer, explorer and florist, in his 1671 publication *The Flower Garden*, makes mention of the cultivation of auriculas. Hughes had, prior to taking up horticulture as a gardener to the Dowager Viscountess Conway, travelled to the West Indies where he learnt about the native flora. His first written work published during his time as gardener for the Viscountess was *The Complete Vineyard* (1665).

Into the 1680s the esteemed Samuel Gilbert, the son-in-law of John Rea, as well as being a Shropshire vicar, wrote and penned his book, *A Florists Vade Mecum*. Gilbert, a florist, wrote that he scorned 'the trifles' – that is thought to mean flowers – adored amongst countrywomen, 'but which were of no esteem to a Florist who is taken up with things of more value'.[3] Gilbert was an auricula enthusiast who owned and ran a small nursery growing anemones amongst the other fashionable flowers of the day.

Auriculas were increasing in value at this time, particularly the more scarce types of cultivars. Double and striped auriculas were worth as much as £20 per plant, which then would have been an enormous sum of money. As well as auriculas, Gilbert grew twenty kinds of anemone, and he was proud to claim that among the plants he grew were some of the best not yet readily available in England.

Richard Bradley, FRS (1688–1732) was Professor of Botany at the University of Cambridge where he wrote numerous books on gardening subjects, including *New Improvements of Planting and Gardening* published in 1726. In this work he mentioned that there were numerous auricula varieties around and that some prominent men of the day had their names attached to many of these varieties.

During the mid-eighteenth century the four 'Florist's Flowers' grown as much as possible to perfection were the anemone, carnation, ranunculus and tulip. These were now joined by a new stablemate, the auricula.

One school of thought, as previously mentioned, was that auriculas found their way to England by way of Flemish weavers who brought them from Flanders whilst escaping persecution and wars during the 1570s. But it seems likely that the auricula was subject to plant exchanges between English florists and their continental counterparts and found their way to these shores by way of this trade. Although Flemish weavers had been working in the south-east of England from the 1300s, it seems that it was the descendents of the contingent that settled in the northern English counties of Lancashire, Cheshire and Yorkshire that practised the art of auricula floristry with such great enthusiasm.

Form, harmony, colour and uniformity were the main considerations for judgng auriculas.

Whether it was just to relieve the drudgery and toil of their work or if it was for the challenge of producing perfect flowers, the weavers, mill workers and others, including gentlemen of 'good fortune', sought to grow auriculas to perfection. It was during the early eighteenth century that the border, self and striped auriculas were joined by the green-edged type of auricula. The edges quickly became very sought after and these were to become the predominant cultivated auricula type.

Meetings of florists would take place at various rendezvous throughout the towns. Inns and market halls would see gatherings where auriculas would be judged on colour, their general form and the proportions of the pips (individual florets). Competitiveness was keen with the main prize often being a copper kettle, a sought-after piece of invaluable culinary equipment; during the mid- seventeenth century the prizes were likely to be a silver spoon or ladle. The prize of a kettle had the added benefit of being practical in the cultivation of auriculas. A kettle was, and still is, a very good vessel for watering potted auriculas, allowing the direction of water flow to be accurately aimed to avoid splashing the auricula foliage, which all too often leads to rot and the probable death of the affected auriculas. Exchanges of auriculas took place much as they do today at regional meetings; some florists would arrive carrying their prized potted blooms on stages (rows of shelves) strapped to their backs and pots of auriculas would be passed around for close scrutinization. As well as auriculas other flowers such as tulips, primulas and carnations had their shows too.

In order to show off their fine plants the development of wooden staging, on which auriculas were grown, was improved by using good quality timber, often painting it with stylized flower portraits or swirls and so on – the auricula theatre was born! Auricula theatres were constructed of wooden shelves that were sometimes stepped and were supported by wooden sides, a base and roof; some elaborate theatres even had a tiled roof! Often the back would be draped with a dark-coloured length of velvet curtain, mainly black, to show off the auriculas to their best advantage by providing a colour contrast. Mirrors were also sometimes attached to the sides in order to further enhance the display.

Issac Emmerton, Jr (1769–1823) of Barnet, North London, is reputed have paid to Mr George Medcalfe of Salford, near Manchester, the comparatively modest sum of 2 British Guineas, which in today's terms equates to around £100 for a single auricula plant. The plant was a specimen of the grey-edge variety 'Lancashire Hero'. Emmerton, who inherited a tree and shrub nursery on his father's death in 1788, was, like his father, a great admirer of auriculas and advocated his own revolting sounding auricula compost comprising bullocks' blood, yellow loam (from mole hills), night soil (a euphemism for human faeces), bakers' scum, sugar, sand and goose dung. This compost recipe sounds absolutely terrible but the mixture was thought to have produced many show winners. Other ingredients would also include sheeps' blood, poultry dung and hay litter. Emmerton was the author of *Plain Treatise on the Culture of Auriculas* published in 1816.

Around the end of the nineteenth century there was a wane of interest in florists' flowers and consequently many excellent named auricula varieties were lost to cultivation forever. However, interest in cultivation saw a renaissance with the alpine type of auricula becoming increasingly popular. It was at this time that a national society was formed and exhibitions, shows and talks were henceforth regulated.

James Douglas, who was head gardener at Loxford Hall

Two Plant Hunters of the Nineteenth Century

- Scotsman Robert Fortune (1812–80) was a well-travelled plant hunter who visited the Far East on several occasions in search of new plants to bring back to the West. He collected and introduced azaleas, camellias, euonymus, forsythia species, hostas, rhododendrons and rosa species.
- Englishman Ernest Wilson (1876–1920) was an avid collector mainly of woody plant subjects. He is thought to have introduced around two thousand plant species including abelias, abies, many different acers, betula species, clematis *armandii* and *montana*, willows and many more.

in Ilford, Essex, published his book *Hardy Florists' Flowers* in 1880. Through this publication he was endeavouring to satisfy the need of those wanting to cultivate auriculas, with information on how to do this successfully. The very important requirement of protecting the show varieties from the elements, in particular rainfall, was discussed. The need for these types to be cultivated in crude frames or under glass was of paramount importance in order to keep the foliage in best condition. The matter of watering was also written about, with the emphasis placed on careful watering by using a watering can fitted with an elongated spout in which a narrowed aperture had been bored, in

order to avoid splashing the foliage of adjacent auriculas. The diameter of the aperture was a similar size to the end of a goose's quill.

The National Auricula Society was founded in 1872–3. With the support of the Manchester Botanical Council the first exhibition of the National Auricula Society was held on Tuesday 29 April 1873. The prizes at this first show were of cash and appear to have been extremely generous. The Class A category was for six dissimilar show varieties, one at least in each of the classes of green-edged, grey-edged, white-edged or self, with a first prize of sixty shillings (£3). In the single plant classes the premium prize was ten shillings (50p) and the first prize was eight shillings (40p) – even those prizes would be more than a lot of people could earn in a week.

The old-time auricula varieties have such thought-provoking and fascinating names. Many had the name of the breeder first followed by the name of their particular hero or heroine in society. The following is a small selection but a more comprehensive list is available in the appendix:

- Archer's Champion of England
- Clough's Jingling Johnny
- Glory of Bolton
- Lord Lascelles
- Owen's Princess of Wales
- Pott's British Champion
- Taylor's Plough Boy
- Whitacker's Rule All
- Wild's Highland Lass

All of the above cultivars are a mixture of edged auriculas, selfs, alpines and striped auriculas; most were of the edged types and a smaller proportion selfs, striped and alpines. It is during more modern times that many more alpines have been raised.

It was what we refer to today as the show varieties that were all important. The edges, particularly the green edges, were coveted by the latter-day florist. As stated earlier it was the northern trio of counties of Lancashire, Cheshire and Yorkshire that became the centre of auricula enthusiasm, in particular Manchester and its surrounding towns of Middleton, Partington, Eccles, Rochdale, Ashton under Lyne and others. Shows were well supported and many old and new fine cultivars were shown.

In order to add 'professionalism' to the art of auricula culture a system of standards was set down in order to select the very best in each class. This became known as The Characteristics of Excellence, which describes the basic parts of an auricula flower:

- The *tube* is the very centre of the flower.
- The *thrum* is the collective term for the parts of fructification in the centre of the *tube*.
- The *paste* is the white colour around the tube or eye of the flower.
- The *ground colour* is the distinctive colour of the flower.

- The *edge* is the outer colour of the flower.
- A *pip* is a single flower.
- A *truss* is several pips with their footstalks (flower stem).

It was deemed that:

- The pip should be round, large, with firm and fleshy petals with no notches or serrations and perfectly flat. The tube should not exceed one fourth of the diameter of the pip of a fine lemon or yellow colour, perfectly rounded and well filled with the anthers or thrum.
- The paste to be perfectly circular, smooth and a dense pure white (yellow in alpines), without crack or other blemish and form a band not less than half the width of the tube.
- The ground colour should be dense and a perfect circle next to the eye, and the darker and richer the better. The outer edge should be a clear unchangeable (uniform) green, grey or white and the same width as the ground colour, which must in no part go through to the edge. From the edge of the paste to the outer edge of the flower should be as wide as from the centre of the tube to the outer edge of the paste.[4]

Standards were also laid down for the plant itself, with attention to the stems, footstalks and the uniformity of the pips.

FORM, HARMONY, COLOUR AND UNIFORMITY

There were four main considerations for the judging of auriculas, as follows:

Form

- The pip's margins should not be undulated or frilled.
- The segments of the corolla should not be too wide.
- The flower should be flat-shaped instead of cup.
- The tube should be perfectly round.
- There should be no cracks in the paste.
- The anthers or thrum should not fill the tube cavity.
- There should be no injuries to the corolla or pip.

Harmony

- The eye or paste should be blemish-free.
- The edge of grey, green or white should be distributed in equal proportions.

Colour

- The depth or intensity of colour should have preference.
- The purest the white, the darker the body colour, the more distinct the margin, the more the merit of the flower.

Uniformity

- The pips should be equal in size.

There were regional variations as to the quantity of pips in each truss shown. In the north of the country anywhere between three and nine pips where shown, whereas in the London area seven was the norm.

During the seventeenth and eighteenth centuries the auricula was well established as a favourite florists' flower and many fine oil paintings of auriculas depicting their rich colours and subtle hues were being produced by Flemish and British artists. In later years auricula images began to be featured on tapestries, postcards and chinaware as their popularity remained high and they became embedded into the consciousness of flower lovers.

The quiet, charming and diminutive book *Alpenblumenfibel* (1936) by Dr Walter Amstutz and Walter Herdeg describes the *P. auricula* as: 'FELSEN-AURIKEL (PRIMULA AURICULA L.) Auch Fluhblume ganannt. Dicke und fleischige Blätter, deren Ränder mehlig gesprenkelt sind. Knallgelb leuchtende Blume, süflich riechend. In Felsritzen wachsend. Kalkliebend. Mancherorts selten, anderorts gehäuft. 1000–1900m.' My apologies for what might be a ropey translation, but the text is partially in old German: 'An early flowering plant of fleshy, thick leaves, off white speckled edges with sweet smelling bright yellow flowers, growing in fissures, and prefers chalky conditions'.[5]

In summary, the auricula has had a quite fascinating history and today still enchants people when seeing the glory of the flower for the first time. This love is still very evident among auricula aficionados. Auricula culture has stood the test of time and will in all probability continue to do so *ad infinitum*.

Auriculas in the World of Art

For their beauty, form and variety, auriculas have captured the imagination of many people from all walks of life, from their first discovery and later from their introduction to the European mainland and the British Isles. A number of talented painters have captured the beauty of auriculas through the ages; many of these artists are European and my research shows several British artists being commissioned to undertake painting auriculas or flower displays in general. The following describes some of the works of those artists depicting auriculas in their paintings and illustrations.

Alexander Marshal (1620–82) was a self-taught, but highly skilled, botanical artist, horticulturalist, seedsman and entomologist. His masterpiece *Florilegium* is furnished with paintings of 284 plant species, amongst which are forty-five anemones, sixty carnations and thirty-eight auriculas. The *Florilegium* or 'Flower Book' was an illustrated work that charted a year in the life of an English garden, from the aconites and snowdrops and crocuses of winter and early spring through to the late-flowering plants such as physalis, *sutherlandia frutescens* and various fruits such as gooseberries, plums and mulberry. The book was celebrated for the vividness of the fine colouring of the artwork produced by Marshal.

Alpine auricula 'Skylark'.

The materials he prepared and used for his paintings were mineral or vegetable pigments. The latter were obtained from flowers, roots and berries and the minerals he used included verdigris, terre-verte and gamboge. Marshal employed the technique of applying watercolours onto paper and then applying transparent washes before sometimes finishing with a layer of gum Arabic, which gave a particularly vivid finish.

Marshal lived in London at various locations, and at one point was lodging in a house belonging to plant hunter and collector John Tradescant the Younger. Marshal also produced numerous watercolours of insects such as butterflies, caterpillars, spiders, crickets and beetles. As if that were not enough, he was also a portrait miniaturist; but he was best known for his plant and flower illustrations.

The majority of Marshal's auricula watercolours are of the striped kinds, which were being produced avidly at this time through selective breeding. During his time he saw the introduction to these isles of many new bulbs, seeds and tubers – an exciting time indeed for the plant portraitist. Among his works were paintings of anemones, which were introduced to these isles during the late 1500s; Marshall is credited with breeding different anemone cultivars himself. Anemones were colloquially known as wind flowers around this time.

Alpine auricula 'Erica'.

In 1675 Marshal was residing at Fulham Palace with his friend Henry Compton (1632–1713), the then Bishop of London, who, apart from his ecclesiastical duties was also a botanist. It was from here, where the Bishop built up a collection of more than one thousand species of plants, that Alexander Marshall was able to paint his plant portraits. In later years his eyesight deteriorated to such an extent that he was unable to paint watercolours and so switched to oils. His *Flowers in a Delft Jar*, which is part of the Paul Mellon collection housed in New Haven in America, depicts a salmon-coloured rose, a yellow carnation and two auriculas. The auriculas painted are border types, one of which is red and the other yellow and grey. Marshall painted what he observed honestly, that

is, he painted the plant as it was presented to him, insect damage and none-too-perfect foliage as it occurred. This was not necessarily his leitmotif but it was for the brilliance of the colours and accuracy that he will be remembered.

The Nuremberg-born German artist Barbara Regina Dietzsch (1706–83) was a fine painter of animals and flowers. In her work *Bouquet Flower Study with Auriculas and Lady Bug*, blue auriculas are set in a small bouquet of five flowers with a descending ladybird, set against a dark brown or black backdrop. Her method of painting was often gouache on vellum, as used in this study, which is composed with attention paid to detail and colours of the flowers and foliage in botanical classification style. Another of her works depicts a pink auricula gathered together with narcissus and a red anemone, and the bouquet tied with a pale blue ribbon. Overall Dietzsch produced more than one hundred works of birds, insects and flowers using the gouache-on-vellum technique.

Georg Dionysus Ehret (1708–70) was a botanist and entomologist, and is best known for his wonderful botanical illustrations. Ehret was born in Germany to a draughtsman and gardener, Ferdinand Christian Ehret, and his wife Anna. Georg Ehret began his career as an apprentice gardener near Heidelberg and he later went on to become a botanical illustrator and worked with noted botanist Carl Linnaeus (1707–78) and George Clifford (1685–1760). Some of his earliest illustrations were in association with Clifford and Linnaeus, as seen in the famous *Hortus Cliffortianus* of 1737 which came to be regarded as a *magnum opus* of horticultural creative writing. It was earlier than this in 1728 when, down on his luck, Ehret met pharmacist and botanist *Johann Wilhelm Weinmann* (1683–1741). Weinmann was practising his trade in Regensburg when he saw some examples of Ehret's work; impressed, he hired him to draw a thousand illustrations to be completed in a year for which he would be paid fifty thaler (a German silver coin). At the end of the year, however, Ehret had not completed his commission and so Weinmann paid him twenty thaler and dismissed him. Later

Ehret tried to sue Weinmann, unsuccessfully.

Ehret found his way to England in 1736; he had great success and eventually became the foremost botanical illustrator of his day. In 1757 he was elected as a Fellow of the Royal Society. Much of his work is to be found in the Natural History Museum in London, the Victoria and Albert Museum, the Lindley Library at the Royal Horticultural Society, the Royal Society, Kew Gardens and the Royal Botanic Gardens. His watercolours-on-vellum technique suited his fine auricula subjects very well and his reputation increased because of his realistic paintings of auriculas.

The Lindley Library

The Royal Horticultural Society's Lindley Library in London and Wisley, Surrey, has gardening literature dating to the early sixteenth century. Also to be found at this great resource are art works and pictures of plants as well as books, journals and garden plans. RHS members are entitled to borrow books on a library basis. Prints of flower illustrations, including old auricula cultivars such as Cockup's Eclipse, Gorton's Champion and Slater's Cheshire Hero, can be purchased through the library.

Amsterdam-based Dutch artist Jan van Huysum (1682–1749) was a celebrated still-life painter who specialized in a highly detailed and colourful style. His work *Flowers in*

a Terracotta Vase depicts a rich assortment of twelve flowers including auriculas, appleblossom, African marigolds, hyacinths, iris, marigolds, narcissi, peonies, poppies, tulips, roses and ranunculus. The flowers in this work are placed in a terracotta vase and are standing in front of an olive-coloured backdrop.

Another Dutch artist Jan van Os (1714–1808) was a painter of botanical subjects and specialized in sumptuous floral arrangements. His detailed work *Carnations, Morning Glory, Roses, Auriculas, Hyacinths and other flowers with a Bird's nest on a Marble Ledge* depicts two trusses of green-edged auriculas that hold their own in the work rather than being swamped by the other larger flowers.

Another Amsterdam-based artist, Paulus Theodorous van Brussel (1754–95), in his work *Flowers in a Vase* painted a collection of flowers including irises, peonies, tulips, roses and auriculas. The flowers are situated in a terracotta vase on a plinth and are of exceptionally vivid colours. The van Brussel style of painting is after Jan van Huysum.

Arguably the finest botanical illustrator of all time was Belgian-born Pierre Joseph Redouté (1759–1840). Famed for his numerous paintings of exotic plants, he is best known for his illustrations of roses and lilies. However a famous painting entitled *Oreilles D'ours and Primula Auricula* depicts a yellow and white butterfly on top of a posy of a yellow-and-red-striped auricula and a deep blue and red alpine auricula. Another of his works featuring the auricula is the painting *Peonies, Cyclamen and Auriculas*, which depicts two trusses of auriculas with a single leaf. One truss is of a blue alpine and the other of a gold-centred deep red auricula.

Danish artist Johan Laurentz Jensen (1800–56) depicted, in typical bold style, two trusses of auriculas in his celebrated canvas *Pansies, Appleblossom, Gloxinia and Primula Auricula* of 1835. He was a productive still-life artist specializing in painting flowers and fruits. This particular canvas sees the group of flowers laying on what appears to be a slab of rustic brown marble in front of olive/brown walling. The scene also includes a small beech tree twig showing the typical yellow/green foliage of the spring season; the pink-tinged appleblossom dominates the centre of the picture and the bi-coloured pansies of maroon and yellow are quite charmingly just drooping over the edge of the slab.

British artist Philip Reinagle (1749–1833) was originally a portrait painter but changed genre to paint animal subjects, landscapes and botanical paintings. He exhibited at the Royal Academy from 1773 onwards and was elected an Associate in 1797. His work *A Group of Auriculas* depicts two green-edged auricula plants in bloom with a backdrop of an Alpine mountain range and, nearer, a stand of conifers. This work was later engraved by Thomas Sutherland (1785–1838). It was Dr Robert

Thornton (1768–1837) in his book *The Temple of Flora: Garden of Nature, with Picturesque Botanical Plates of the new Illustration of the Sexual System of Linnaeus*, who employed Reinagle as one of the two designers for his work.

Another well-known British artist of flower portraits was H.G. Moon (1857–1905). Moon was born in Barnet, near London, and excelled as a young artist but took up a place in law as a clerk with the eventual aim of practising law. However, the call of art and horticulture saw him take up a position with *The Garden* publication during 1880. This popular horticultural publication was edited and founded by William Robinson (1838–1935) and Moon's works shown in it were thought of very highly. During his time, Moon

produced many fine drawings of flowers, including the work *Auricula Mrs Moore + Prince of Greens + Charles Perry* in 1887. Auricula 'Mrs Moore' is a grey-edged show auricula, which is bunched together with 'Prince of Greens', a green-edged show auricula and 'Charles Perry', which is either a dark blue alpine or a self. None of these varieties appear to be in cultivation today. Moon was renowned for the highly realistic paintings of his subjects and, in particular, his watercolours of orchids for which he undertook many commissions.

During the Victorian/ Edwardian era the practice of painting garden scenes was well established; the preceding garden art had been mainly about the landscape with not much produced in the way of the colour of flowers. The

Alpine auricula 'Kercup'.

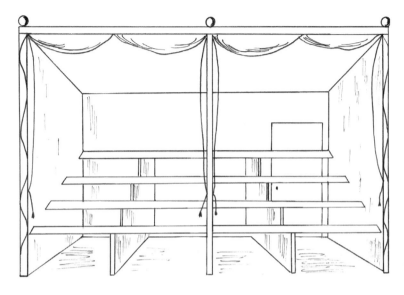

Impression of old auricula theatre.

Dylan, The Beatles, model Jean Shrimpton and members of the Royal Family.

McEwen produced beautiful watercolours of many flowers and amongst the auriculas he painted were the cultivars 'S.G. Holden', a white edge, 1963, which is a watercolour on vellum; 'Gold of Ophir', a yellow self, 1963, again a watercolour on vellum; and 'Lady Drury', a light-centred alpine. None of these cultivars appear to be in cultivation today, but all are as lovely as many newer, similar-looking modern ones. The auricula paintings McEwen produced were done on commission for garden writer C. Oscar Moreton. Arguably unsurpassed in their beauty, McEwen supplied seventeen colour plates of auriculas that were included in Moreton's 1964 book *The Auricula: Its History and Character*.

THE AURICULA THEATRE

Many people have heard the name or term 'Auricula Theatre' but have not had the great pleasure of actually seeing one housing a colourful auricula display in the spring. The very name conjures up in the imagination of keen gardeners a feeling of illusion or magic being employed to entrance the viewer of flowering auriculas.

It is not only gardeners who are aware of auricula theatres, however. Increasingly the general public are becoming aware of auricula displays. Perhaps the most commonly encountered auricula theatre today is a simple purpose-made

cottage garden style of painting as represented by George Claude Strachan (1865–1935) depicted the popular herbaceous flowering plants of the period growing on the walls of and in the typical English cottage garden. The well-kept cottage gardens that he painted in watercolour showed phlox, asters, poppies and the ubiquitous hollyhocks standing on guard next to front doors. Auriculas would probably have been a part of the scene but, of course, the flowers would have been spent before the summer-flowering favourites took over the horticultural interest. Scotsman Strachan lived in Liverpool after leaving his native Edinburgh, and exhibited much of his prolific output there at the Walker Art Gallery.

Coming closer to the present day celebrated artist Rory McEwen (1932–82)

was a botanical artist and folk singer. Born the son of a renowned Scottish politician, he served with the Queen's Own Cameron Highlanders in Egypt. After his distinguished military career he began to paint and publish his watercolours of flowers, leaves, fruit and vegetables, many of which are displayed in the Scottish National Gallery, and the Fitzwilliam Museum, Cambridge. Many more of his works are held in private collections. As well as a talented artist, McEwen was a renowned folk singer; for his musical talent he appeared often on the television programme *Tonight*, playing and singing traditional Scottish folk songs and ditties. Across the Atlantic he did a stint on the *Ed Sullivan Show*. Living the life he did in London he met many celebrities including Bob

wooden cabinet for the display of auriculas during the spring flowering time. The theatres not only display the plants but also act as protection from the elements. The farina of the show types is easily ruined by rainfall, and laying water on the crown of auriculas can cause rot and ultimately death.

Auricula theatres, or stages as they were sometimes known, have been in use in Great Britain since the eighteenth century. Auricula-exhibiting miners and weavers would strap their small home-made auricula theatres to their backs and pedal off on their bicycles to florists' venues, which were often taverns or town halls and similar places. Here they would display their plants and, hopefully, win prizes.

Structurally the auricula theatres are similar to a set of bookshelves but some have certain differences such as tiered shelving, twin hinged doors and quite often a backcloth of dark green or black velvet to show off the colourful auricula flowers to best effect. Apart from these fairly simple theatres there were, at one time, elaborate structures such as at Calke Abbey, Derbyshire (still in use today), which were constructed to house a very large display of auriculas. This particular auricula theatre was constructed by the estate carpenter in 1857 and was at first referred to as a 'verandah', only a few years later becoming known as an auricula theatre. This particular auricula theatre is 19ft in length by 4ft in depth and stands at 9ft in height. It

still stands today, displaying some 200 to 250 flowering auriculas each spring.

Significant Events in 1857

- The Indian Rebellion, also known as the Indian mutiny, started in Meerut.
- The Art Treasures Exhibition was held at Old Trafford Botanical Gardens.
- Botanist and gardener John Lindley was created a Fellow of the Linnean Society.
- Joseph Conrad, the famous novelist, was born in the Ukraine.
- The world's oldest football club, Sheffield United, was formed.
- *The Handbook of Fruit Culture* was published. Author Thomas Gregg describes the correct method for the management of fruit trees.

Auricula theatres were thought to have been in use at Badminton House in Gloucester and Beaufort House in Chelsea, London, under the ownership of the Duchess of Beaufort, where Mary Somerset had her large collections of auriculas. Whether these were for private viewing only is a moot point, as surely the owners of such an extensive collection of auriculas would want to show them off to other members of the gentry, the clergy and interested florists of the region. It is quite likely that there would have been many large auricula theatres dotted around the country in stately piles but, sadly, these have all but disappeared.

The auriculas were displayed

in traditional 'Long Tom' pots and similar-sized clay flower pots. They were placed on tiered shelving giving the best viewing perspective and also allowing the plants to receive the best light levels. The auriculas would have been sited elsewhere in gardens or nurseries when not in flower, perhaps in frames, and put into the auricula theatres for display purposes from late March onwards. Auricula theatres or stages have been the ideal way in which to give an opinion as to the merits of the displayed plants. From the viewings the colour of the flowers and foliage would be appraised as to the suitability of some of the auriculas to be used as future seed parents.

A roof and side walls on the theatres were essential in order to offer protection from the elements and drapes in the front and back were used by some to keep out frost and wind, unless large garden walls afforded this protection (as at Calke Abbey). Such is the size of the theatre at Calke Abbey that the two hundred or so auriculas displayed at any one time is quite a spectacle.

Of course the scale of the Calke Abbey auricula theatre is exceptional, as it is believed there were numerous more modest theatres or stages to house the gentry's collections throughout the British Isles. Research shows that some were highly ornate with pictures of rural scenes of flora and fauna painted on them, and some had velvet drapes or sawn wooden 'curtains' attached to the front sides to imitate real curtains. Mirrors too were sometimes attached and used as side walls to enhance the display by deception or illusion. There were also the more modest affairs of planks of wood made in bookcase style constructed by the working-man florist. They were attached to external house walls and temporarily removed to take to shows where they would be free standing for the duration. One can imagine a scene of a simple lead-roofed auricula stage sited on the external wall of a back-to-back terraced property being taken down, loaded carefully with the grower's prized auriculas and off the owner would pedal with his valuable load to show off his auriculas at a local show.

Displaying auriculas for possible sale or for effect was also common practice during the early years of auricula culture. In his book *New Improvements of Planting and Gardening* Richard Bradley says that pots of auriculas should be in a sunny part of the garden. He believed the morning sun to be particularly favourable to them. He also mentioned the farina by calling it a dust that contributed to their beauty. The importance of shelter against rain that would ruin the colours of the auriculas was another concern.

It was not just in Great Britain that auricula theatres were used; in France, Belgium and Germany too, structures both elaborate and simple were also in common use. Articles and certain publications that have survived the years tell us that auricula culture was practised extensively in some regions of northern France and Flanders in Belgium. It is thought that it was here that flower theatres were first made in the seventeenth century to protect the delicate flowers of carnations, tulips and auriculas from the wind and rain and for the purpose of showing them. The auricula theatres were of twofold usefulness: they were constructed to protect the blooms and delicate farina of the mealed auricula types and they were also used for display and sale purposes.

Abbé Samson-François Guénin, of whom little is known except that he was 'Directeur des Aydes' in Amiens and an auricula enthusiast, is attributed with the treatise entitled *Traité de la Culture Parfait de l'Oreilles d'Ours ou Auricule*. It was first published anonymously in 1732. (The 1735 edition states the book was published in Brussels by Chez Henry Frikx, but it was in fact printed in France. Guénin notes in the preface that the first edition of 1732 had a very small print run, due to the printer's doubt that the work would prove of interest.) This work shows how the sometimes tantalizing and delicate auricula flower had recently become exceptionally popular among the *curieux* (those of an enquiring mind).

In the publication Guénin lists more than twenty pages of the names and locations of auricula growers, who were mainly local *dignitaires, abbaés* and *supériers* with whom he was acquainted in northern France and the Low Countries. Guénin also gives a lot of advice on auricula cultivation and expresses his own love of the flowers and to this end several poems were written. The 1735 second edition features an enchanting frontispiece of an auricula florist proudly displaying his twenty or so potted auriculas – accompanied by several small rodents! A banner reads, '*Chacun Aime, Entretient Les Siens. L'Auricule Nourit Les Miens.*' Roughly translated from the historical French this is 'Each likes to maintain their auriculas in their own way.'

There is a wonderful drawing featured in the 1738 edition of Guénin's book, the top portion of which shows thirty flowering potted auriculas on a stage in three staggered rows under a banner that reads '*Chacun A Sa Marotte*'; roughly, 'Each one (everyone) to their own hobby'. There are three smiling joker busts, two on plinths to each side of the stage and one in the centre looking down on the display. The bottom portion of the picture is of a centrally placed flowering auricula on a small plinth with an upward-looking and smiling joker's bust beneath. The middle ground of the picture is of ornamental flower beds with either manicured lawns or walkways between. The background sees a hedge with a portico that leads to an area of columnar-shaped trees. To me it seems the top portion of the drawing is the central part of a free-standing auricula theatre, probably constructed and carved from hard wood, perhaps oak. This stylized theatre adds to the mystery and veneration the auricula had during those times.

Back in Great Britain John Abercrombie (1726–1806) co-authored a book with Thomas Mawe and other gardeners entitled, *Every Man His Own Gardener being a new and much more complete Gardener's Kalender than any one hitherto published*. He says that during the month of April, 'Auriculas will now blow and care must be taken to protect the curious sorts in pots, from rain and wind and also from too much sun.'[6] The authors go on to say that the farina or, rather quaintly, mealy dust, that overspreads the surface of the flowers contributes to their beauty and care should be taken in order to protect it from inclement weather: 'Let the pots, therefore, as the flowers open, be immediately removed and placed on the shelves of the auricula theatre, or where the flowers may be protected occasionally from such weather as would deface the bloom.'[7] They talk about the stand or stage as having three to five or six ranges of shelves of around 6in wide.

Some auriculas were grown in larger pots than they are today, which explains the somewhat excessive width of the shelves. The shelves would rise theatrically above each other from the front. The importance of protection over the top at all times is stated in *Every Man His Own Gardener*, with occasional protection of the sides and front by temporary use of canvas or mats (curtains). It goes on to say that when the air is sharp (frosty), or in high winds and driving rain the curtains 'must be let down' and removed when the weather improved, and to remain open constantly. Abercrombie and Mawe beseech their readers to check the displayed auriculas every day for water requirements. They advise not to let water fall on the flowers for fear of 'defacing their beauty' and recommend moderate watering. The importance of keeping the pots neat and free from weeds and also from 'decayed' leaves is stressed: 'By thus placing your auriculas on a covered stage it not only preserves the flowers much longer in beauty but you also more readily view them and they show themselves to much greater advantage than when placed on the ground.'[8]

John Abercrombie's Book on Fruit Trees

In 1779 noted gardener and garden writer John Abercrombie published his seminal work on fruit tree culture, *The British Fruit Gardener*. The book instructed on the approved methods of planting and cultivating fruit trees. The practice of pruning top fruit trees in order to achieve the finest crops was detailed, as were instruction on budding and grafting. He gave information on the care of the almond tree, the apple tree, cherry trees, grape vines, medlars, nectarines, raspberries and walnuts, among others.

Research shows that the monks of the Abbey of Tournei in Belgium grew such a vast amount of auriculas that it required no less than fifteen auricula theatres in order to display them all. Biffen, in *The Auricula* (1951) says, 'In Holland also many new sorts were being raised, some of which found a ready market here, whilst in Germany there were so many that F.A. Kannegieser (*Aurikel Flora nach der Natur gemahlt*, 1801) was able to figure 144 of them.'[9] By around 1820 the cultivation of auriculas on the continent had become so popular that in order to show them off to their neighbours and friends growers constructed, or had constructed for them, purpose-made auricula theatres or stages.

Biffen goes on to describe that the stages to which the auriculas were transferred from the growing frames, when flowering was imminent, were permanent wooden structures that were opened to the north aspect. They had a watertight roof with ventilators at the sides. Very often the back was painted using a dark colour in order to display the colourful flowering auriculas to best effect. It is also noted that some exhibitors had a painted landscape theme instead of the usual dark background. Biffen also observes that, '… as a final refinement, mirrors were attached to the sides to give the impression of greater size to the exhibit'.[10] The auricula theatres had two or three shelves assembled in a staircase fashion, that is, staggered vertically. The plant pots may also have been painted a shade of green to disguise the sometimes discordant terra cotta colour.

During this time very many auriculas were being cultivated and a preponderance of flower shows to support this culture were staged. In Great Britain the majority of these shows were held in the three northern English counties of Cheshire, Lancashire and southern Yorkshire. Whilst London also had numerous flower shows, many small towns and villages had auricula shows that were staged in nurseries, public houses and even on occasion in private residences.

Frames were used to house auriculas and were constructed mainly for cultivation but also, to an extent, for viewing. These frames would often be mounted on legs, and sometimes placed on top of brick piles, in order to facilitate this dual purpose. According to George W. Johnson (1802–1886) in *The Gardener's Monthly Volume* the legs were between 2ft and 3ft high. The dimensions of the frame he describes are: overall width 7ft 2in; 4ft 8in the back height; 3ft 8in front height and 3ft 8in depth. Johnson goes on to give other dimensions of these frames. He mentions the 2in rise between the 5in-width shelves. There was sometimes extra boarding of deal wood around the frames to give more stability in stormy weather.[11]

Johnson was referring to the dimensions of a purpose-made auricula frame as employed by the late Dr Horner of Hull, who regarded as one of the most successful auricula cultivators. He says of the winter months:

> The winter, or a period of rest – the objects to be attained at this time of their cultivation, is freedom from excessive wet, protection from intense frost, and the admission of air freely. This period extends from the close of October, or beginning of November, according to the severity of the season may begin, early or late, to the end of January.[12]

It is clear from the above that a lot of care and trouble, probably born from experience, was employed in order to house auriculas in a safe manner. Frost protection and adequate ventilation was considered. The 'top lights' were propped open by utilizing an iron bar that had holes along it at 2in or 3in intervals. A strategically placed nail projecting from the sash would locate in one or other of the holes. The front of the frame had two hinged sashes, which would be let down to allow good ventilation. The ends of the frame were also of glass, '...and in the back, which is wood, there is a door for the convenience of getting to the pots behind, and also for thorough ventilation.'[13]

Regarding the insides of the frame Johnson relates:

> There are five rows of shelves, graduated to the slope of the glass; they have a piece an inch wide sawn out of the middle; there is a space also left between them, so that the bottom of the frame is quite open for the abundant admission of air to circulate thoroughly around the sides and bottom of the pots.

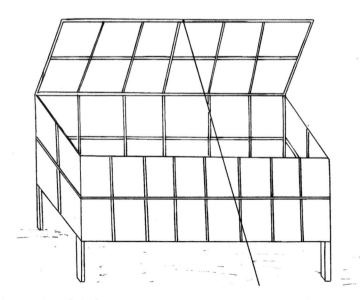

Impression of old frame.

Johnson says that by letting down the front light only the plants may be left for several consecutive days to take advantage of light and air. To benefit from an occasional shower the top lights were removed. As for watering, Johnson tells us of Horner's recommendations. He advocated that watering should be gradually withdrawn so that during the months of December and January the soil is prevented from becoming 'absolutely dry'. He goes on to say that if the soil is kept wet or damp the plants will be in danger of contracting disease and be likely to suffer from frosts. During periods of intense frost the frame and auriculas were protected by using stout blankets of tarpaulin sheet draped over them. He warns that if the plants are not protected in this manner then the flower stems will be found dead or with only two or three pips to show.

Johnson notes that Mr Emmerton moved his auricula plants into their winter quarters earlier than Dr Horner and that he utilized a cucumber frame for this purpose. Johnson felt that as result of this, and the auriculas not being placed in a purpose-made frame, the plants would require much more care. Dr Horner had his frames orientated to the south and placed his plants into them during October.

The hardiness of auriculas is compared to that of the common primrose (*P. vulgaris*), but it is said that they cannot stand the heavy autumn and winter rains that were seen as the greatest enemy of the plant. As we know today, if potted auriculas receive too much water they will rot away all too easily.

These old growers were specific as to the times of the days when lights should be placed on or hinged back into place. During the winter period it was suggested that this covering up for the night should be done at 4 o'clock in the afternoon, and the frames uncovered again at 9 o'clock the next morning. Ventilation was given again then except if there was rain or snow. If this was the case then the covers were removed but the lights left on.

During the turn of the year light frosts were seen as no problem to the plants, but warning was given as to severe frosts which would freeze the mold (compost) in the pots and damage the forming flower trusses. At 3 o'clock the frame covers should put on again for the night and an extra cover of frost protection given. During the latter half of January, if the weather had turned mild and if the auriculas were very dry, they would be given water or allowed to have three hours of moderate rain, providing this rain came from the south-west aspect. This practice would be 'repeated every opportunity till the mold has got moderately moist'.[14]

Notably there were cultivable variations among auricula growers on some points of husbandry. For instance, Mr Douglas advocated frames should face to the south during the winter months and face north from May to October.

Auriculas were not the only flowering plant to be displayed in auricula theatres. In many cases carnations or pinks were housed just before flowering time, as were potted hyacinths, tulips, polyanthus, anemones and ranunculas. From around 1800 it became fashionable to bring flowers into domestic dwellings for everyone to enjoy interior flower displays.

As alluded to before, the rise in popularity of auriculas in Great Britain again over the past few years has caused, not surprisingly, a renewed interest in auricula theatres; over the centuries many different designs were prevalent but all had the common theme of displaying auriculas to best advantage for the viewer and florist alike. There are a handful of organizations that offer auricula theatre displays during the spring. These are generally auricula nurseries and these events are well worth seeking out to experience flowering auriculas en masse. As well as at Calke Abbey there are auricula theatres at the Museum of Wales at Carmarthen, the Easton Walled Gardens near Grantham in Lincolnshire and the Museum of Garden History in London. The latter venue gives an opportunity to see show auriculas displayed in the traditional manner in an elaborate auricula theatre, designed for the museum by the Dowager Marchioness of Salisbury.

Alpine auricula 'Alf'.

2 Types of Auriculas

The auricula is divided into different types for exhibition purposes and also to place these different types in defined categories for collections. These categories are: the alpines, the borders, the double auricula and the show auriculas. The show type comprises the edges, the fancies, the selfs and, finally, the striped auriculas.

Auricula growers, both professional and amateur, will often have their own personal favourite type, which can sometimes be the type they first came across. A first encounter with the charming auricula may well be at a plant sale, with those for sale at a specialist alpine nursery or a display at a flower show. A large display such as the one put up at the Malvern Spring Flower Show each spring is a magnificent sight to behold. Flowering auriculas are displayed in all their glory and are tended by the country's most eminent growers. The beauty of the velvety petal texture and bright and bold colours combined with the simplicity of the plants is an image not to be forgotten.

The edged types were grown avidly in days of old, and other types have had varied and changed fortunes. Some auricula types were very fashionable for a period of time, and then mysteriously fell out of favour only to return to the forefront at a later time. Today there are far more double types

being grown, of many varied colours. During early times doubles were scarce, probably owing to the greater difficulty in propagation. They have been trickier to use for propagation owing to the double layers of flowers but modern techniques have addressed this problem and there are now far more double cultivars being produced.

There are not as many border types grown in gardens as there once were, and their popularity has never been the same as for the show varieties or alpines. But a renewed interest in popularity has led to an increase in supply of this auricula type. The preferred method of growing the borders these days is as potted specimens in cold greenhouses or frames. They are also very much at home in the garden, planted in beds, borders or rockeries.

ALPINE AURICULAS

The alpines, along with the borders, are widely considered to be the easiest of auriculas to grow successfully and they are therefore an ideal introductory auricula type for beginners. Alpine auriculas have strong constitutions and are quite vigorous growers, thriving in garden borders or alpine beds where the flowers are not easily marred by inclement weather. They are widely grown in cold greenhouses

with maximum ventilation given at all times to allow for good air circulation. In wet weather, however, it is advisable to keep roof vents shut in order to stop the rain falling on any plants that are placed directly beneath vents and causing them to rot due to water splash.

The alpines display an enchanting variety of coloured flowers, including pinks, reds, crimson, orange-to-brown and lavender-to-purple. The petals change from their main colours of darker shades in the centre to lighter shades at the outer edges. Alpines are sub-divided into light-centred or dark-centred; this indicates that the flowers have either white or gold centres respectively.

Foliage is generally a mid-green colour, with the leaves of some different cultivars being quite rounded, whilst some are strap-like, others are pointed and some are serrated, as with cultivar 'Pippin'. The alpines are free from farina in all parts of the plant making them easy to distinguish from the borders, which often have farina in parts. There are well over four hundred cultivars of the alpine auricula in circulation today, some of which are ancient varieties that are still performing well amongst numerous others of varying constitution and beauty.

Selected alpine cultivars
'Alf' tends to be a relatively small plant but the flowers more than make up for what

Alpine auricula 'Argus'.

it lacks in lush foliage with a floriferous flourish at flowering time. The light-centred flowers are pleasantly shaped and have a broad, pale lilac edge. 'Alf' is a reliable alpine that pleases year after year. It is well worth seeking out to add class to any collection.

'Alison Telford' is a gold-centred alpine auricula of a dusky red colour. It is a good performer and readily available from specialist auricula nurseries.

'Amicable' was bred by Derek Telford in 1994 and is a gold-centred alpine of a middle-brown colouring. This cultivar is diminutive and has a tendency to be remontant (having a repeat flowering during the autumn), which can be seen as a bonus.

'Ancient Society' is a lovely gold-centred red and orange alpine named after the Ancient Society of York Florists and is a regular on the show bench. It is a very handsome variety that was first raised by Ken Bowser in 1997, from a cross between alpines 'Sirius' × 'Snooty Fox II'. The Ancient Society of York Florists claims to be the oldest horticultural society in the world, dating back to 1768. Its flower shows include narcissi, tulips, cyclamen, primulas and, of course, auriculas.

'Andrea Julie' is a bright orange red of light shading. It has pert pips on shortish stems. This cultivar was raised by auricula breeder Derek Telford and named after his daughter.

Named after the talented and skilful professional footballer, once of Manchester United and other top clubs, is cultivar 'Andy Cole'. This light-centred purple shaded alpine was bred by Derek Telford during 1983

and took top honours during that year at the Harrogate Spring Show.

'Anwar Sadat', named after the third president of Egypt, is a lovely alpine of blue to mauve. It is a durable auricula that always pleases and should be sought out for addition to a collection.

'Applecross' is still available from some sources of supply. It is closely related to the alpine cultivar 'Sandwood Bay' and was raised originally during 1968. This alpine displays rich red pips on long stems and has been shown numerous times.

A must for the new collector is 'Argus', c.1887 and first shown during 1895. It was bred by Mr J.J. Keen of the southern section of the National Auricula and Primrose Society. This cultivar is of a strong constitution and shows no signs of old age. It was introduced during the period when alpine auriculas were probably at their most popular, from the early 1870s to the early 1900s. 'Argus' was instantly popular and remains so today. It is easy to propagate from as it offsets generously, providing the grower with plenty of material from which to increase stock. The colour is of a plum shading to a wine red. The pips are borne on strong trusses and 'Argus' always draws positive remarks from those seeing it for the first time.

'Arwen' is a plum red alpine raised by J. Radford in 2002. It is a neat, reliable cultivar but produces few offsets.

Also among the light-centred alpine auriculas is 'Avril Hunter'.

A light-centred alpine of purple with blue shades it is a neat plant of smallish trusses but with well-formed pips. It was bred by Derek Telford in 1988.

'Beatrice' is a light-centred blue (horticultural blue) to pale blue alpine. It is not seen as an outstanding auricula but is a very reliable plant with good flowering performance.

'Bilbo Baggins', named after J.R.R. Tolkien's wonderful character from the novel *Lord of the Rings*, was bred by John Radford in 1999. It has won many prizes since its introduction.

'Blue Yodeler' was raised by Ken Bowser in 2001 and sports shades of a velvety bright blue. This fine light-centred auricula was raised from the alpine 'Victoria de Wemyss' from seedlings given by Derek Telford to Jack Wemyss-Cooke.

'Bolero' is a truly lovely gold-centred alpine of coppery red-coloured blooms. It has exceptionally neat trusses and has won top awards. It was bred by C.F. Hill in 1964. 'Bolero' is slow to offset, making it an alpine not too easy to find.

'Bookham Firefly' is an intriguingly named gold-centred alpine of crimson shading to maroon, which was bred in 1936 by James Douglas and is still going strong today. It is a robust grower that offsets quite freely and is still sought after.

'Bradford City' is a fine gold-centred alpine auricula of a deep red or plum colour. This popular alpine was bred by S. Cravens and first appeared in 1996. It is named after the professional football club from

Alpine auricula 'Ancient Society'.

the city in west Yorkshire and bears their colours. It is a pleasant-coloured alpine of reliable performance.

'Cambodunum' is a light-centred purple alpine of good constitution. It is another reliable performer that has great flowering qualities. The plant offsets freely and can get quite

Alpine auricula 'Cambodunum'.

Alpine auricula 'C.W. Needham'.

large in overall size, requiring a 4in pot and perhaps even a half-litre deep plastic pot. 'Cambodunum' is the Roman name for the south-west Bavarian town of Kempten im Allgäu, one of the earliest settlements in Germany.

'Chelsea Bridge' is a light-centred alpine of a lovely blue colour shaded to a purple-blue. It has a light and delicate

Alpine auricula 'Dilly Dilly'.

fragrance and is often in good form.

'Cuddles' is a similar alpine to cultivar 'Ancient Society' but is of darker hues, appearing almost brown. It was first bred by Derek Telford in 1994. It is a strong and vigorous grower that is now appearing more often on nurseries' plants list.

'C.W. Needham' is a lovely dark blue-to-purple light-centred alpine and was bred by Percy Johnson in 1934. It has a lovely pale purple edge that enhances the deep purple of the main colour. It is an auricula of good form and vigorous growth that produces a good quantity of offsets each season. It was named after a noted judge of the northern section of the National Primula and Auricula Society. The flowers are quite a delight and the cultivar is a must for the serious collector.

'Dilemma' is another gold-centred alpine of a bold red colour. This cultivar was bred by Ken Bowser in 2000 and is of a vigorous nature. It is a good example of how the gold and red combination of colours on some of the alpine cultivars can make the particular cultivar really vibrant.

'Dilly Dilly' is a delightful light-centred alpine auricula, bred by Keith Leeming in 1993. It has mid-green leaves and lovely lavender blue flowers that last well and it is a particularly photogenic cultivar. This is a special auricula and much loved by many growers.

'Divint Dunch', bred by Derek Telford in 1990, is named after a phrase translated from a heavy Geordie (Tyneside) accent that reputedly means,

'Don't push'. 'Divint Dunch' has a lovely plum-and-purple colouring.

'Douglas Bader' is a fine alpine auricula of a deep blue and pale blue, bred by Derek Telford in 1995. Named after the Second World War heroic flying ace and great amateur golfer, it is a name that will live on forever in British history. Patriotic auricula growers will want this one in their collection.

'Dusky Maiden' is a gold-centred alpine bred by A. Delbridge in 1987. It is of a brown and purple colour, sometimes appearing to be more like a maroon hue. It is a well-formed cultivar of reliable flowering performance.

'Eastern Promise' is an orangey-red and brown gold-centred alpine bred by Derek Telford in 1995. It is living up to its promise as a very good alpine.

'Eastern Queen' was bred by A. Delbridge in 1988. She is a gold-centred alpine auricula of brown shaded to old gold. 'Eastern Queen' gained premier status when first shown as a seedling.

'Erica' is a statuesque lady. It is a strong-growing, gold-centred and red-flowering auricula created by auricula breeder Gwen Baker in 1984.

'Frank Faulkner' was raised by Frank Faulkner Jr in 1951 from a 'Tom Jones' × 'Irene' cross. This gold-centred alpine is of a dark crimson that shades to a bright red and has a velvety texture.

'Gay Crusader' is noted for the brightness of its colours, which are a very dark crimson and stunning orange. This

Alpine auricula 'Douglas Bader'.

gold-centred alpine was bred by Les Kaye in 1982 from 'Rodeo' × 'Andrea Julie'. 'Gay Crusader' is named after a Derby horse race winner.

'Good Report' was bred by Derek Telford in 1992. It is a light-centred blue alpine and performs consistently. 'Good Report' also offers plenty of offset material for propagation purposes.

Alpine auricula 'Dusky Maiden'.

Alpine auricula 'Habanera'.

'Habanera' is a first-class light-centred alpine of a lovely pinky purple. It was bred by Derek Telford during 1989 and is one of the many fine auriculas introduced by this auricula breeder. This great cultivar is a reliable performer that displays good clear colours with a particularly delicate scent. 'Habanera' is named after the well-known aria from Georges Bizet's opera *Carmen*, sang by famous sopranos such as Maria Callas, Angela Gheorghiu and others. A fine alpine that is that is worthy of a place on any stage.

'Harry Hotspur' sounds like a character from a boys' comic circa the 1950s. This light-centred pink alpine auricula is very reliable and produces good flowers of a delicate fragrance.

'Hazel' displays purple shades and often appears on the show benches. She is of a good constitution and shows well but is not readily available so needs some seeking out.

'Heady' is a light-centred alpine of a lovely pink colour. It was bred by Derek Telford in 1994 and performs well, sending up good trusses of fine form.

'Ian Greville' is an outstanding exhibition variety. It has well-rounded flowers of a beautiful clear pink colour and was bred by Cliff Timpson in 1994. It has gone on to win premier awards and is sure to keep on winning. This lovely alpine auricula is one all keen auricula growers should have in their collection.

'Jeannie Telford' was bred in 1977 by Derek Telford and named after his wife. This light-centred alpine is a dark pink and very prettily shaded.

'Jersey Bounce' is an orange-and-brown alpine auricula bred by Derek Telford in 1998. Is a cultivar of very pleasant fragrance and good looks. 'Jersey Bounce' was a song and an instrumental piece of music performed by Benny Goodman and others.

'Jessie Lightfoot' was bred

Alpine auricula 'Ian Greville'.

by P. Bowen during 2001. It is a gold-centred alpine with a golden brown colour.

'Joe Perks' was introduced in 1993 by Derek Telford. It is a brown flowering alpine that is readily available from several auricula nurseries.

'John Wayne' is a popular award-winning gold-centred alpine, bred by L. Bailey in 1979 by crossing 'Frank Crosland' × 'Joy'. The colour is a lovely pink and plum. It was well acclaimed when it first appeared on the show scene and remains popular today. It offsets well and is a reliable cultivar of good quality.

'Joy', as well as being a parent to 'John Wayne', is a very fine alpine auricula and has won many awards over the years. She was bred by Percy Johnson, a gardener and auricula enthusiast from Altrincham, in Cheshire. The colour is a rich, dark red.

'Katchachurian' was bred in 1992 by Derek Telford and is a bright red colour. It was named after the famous Russian composer Aram Katchachurian (1903–78). It is a bold and strong alpine auricula.

'Kevin Keegan' is a lovely deep pink colour with a bright white centre, named after one of the finest professional footballers this island has produced. It is a well-regarded alpine with a good and loyal following.

'Lee Paul' is a gold-centred alpine of maroon colour but it sometimes looks rather more brown than maroon. It is shaded to yellow or gold and was produced by Derek Telford in 1990 from a seedling from

Alpine auricula 'John Wayne'.

the alpine 'Sirius'. 'Lee Paul' can look very striking when first opening but the blooms tend to change to a duller hue with age. Nevertheless it is a very good alpine and is widely distributed. It is a multi-award winner at the shows and always in good demand.

'Mandarin' is a lovely light-centred alpine of pink shades. It was bred in 1992 by Derek

Alpine auricula 'Lee Paul'.

Alpine auricula 'Margot Fonteyn'.

Telford. It is one of those alpines that pleases without being truly great; a good offsetter and a reliable auricula.

'Margaret Faulkner' is a purple-to-crimson alpine of fine form and for these reasons has been a good show performer. This fine alpine was bred in 1953 by F. Faulkner from 'Gordon Douglas' × 'Joy'.

'Margot Fonteyn' was of course named after the inimitable prima ballerina, one of the finest ballerinas from England. This gold-centred red alpine is of very good form and always gives a star performance.

'Marion Howard Spring' is named after the keen amateur gardener and garden writer who was the wife of famous journalist-turned-novelist Howard Spring. Marion penned the interesting and very readable novel *Memories and Gardens*, which charts her married life with Howard and the gardens they created. Bred by J. Ballard in 1975, Marion Howard Spring is a reddish-pink, gold-centred alpine.

'Pippin' is a very reliable gold-centred alpine and always performs and shows well. It has a colour of shaded maroon-red to light crimson/cherry-red and has a light serration to its leaves. Raised by James Douglas in 1931, it is a strong grower, reliable and offsets well. 'Pippin' deserves to be grown more widely for its many fine attributes. 'Pippin' is, without a doubt, a great favourite of mine.

'Prince John' is an alpine variety from 1916, bred by J. Douglas. It is a gold-centred alpine of maroon colouring that shares the positive characteristics of 'Argus', being a good offsetter and a very tidy and eminently showable plant. It is another good auricula for the novice and often appears on the nursery lists.

'Sandra' is a light-centred alpine that was bred by Hal Cohen in 1973. It is a very neat, tidy and refined flower

Alpine auricula 'Pippin'.

that is easy to grow to a show standard. It was awarded Premier Alpine in 1982.

'Sandwood Bay' is a bright red, gold-centred alpine of distinction. It was bred by D. Edwards *c.*1971 from 'Blossom' × 'Mrs Savory'. It is a lovely vibrant alpine auricula for anyone's collection.

'Sirius' is an eye-catching and popular alpine of maroon or purple colour shaded to cream. It is a quite beautiful plant, easy to grow and offsets freely. It was raised by Frank Jacques in 1971.

'Skylark' is a purple-flowering light-centred alpine bred by Derek Telford in 1992. It is a pleasantly coloured and shaded alpine, often seen with notched petals.

'Snooty Fox' is a dark red-to-orange alpine of a bright nature that was bred by Derek Telford during 1978 from a cross between 'Andrea Julie' and a seedling.

'Sophie' was bred by Ken Bowser and is a pink alpine with very attractive looks. It has nicely formed pips that are held on strong footstalks.

'Stella North' is another lovely pink alpine with purple hints. A popular light-centred auricula bred by D. Skinner in 1993.

'Stella South' is a pale purple alpine of very good form and one worthy of a place in a collection.

'T.A. Hadfield' is a very deep velvety maroon-pink alpine which shades to light pink. It is an auricula of pleasing overall good form and a good offsetter for propagation. 'T.A. Hadfield' was introduced by Derek Telford in 1993.

Alpine auricula 'Sandwood Bay'.

'Vee Too' is a light-centred purple blue alpine that was produced by way of a seedling crossed with 'Paragon'. It was bred by A. Hawkes in 1967.

Another lovely lady is 'Victoria de Wemyss'. This fine alpine was raised by Jack Wemyss-Cooke from a tray of auricula seedlings that were given to him by Derek Telford

Alpine auricula 'Sirius'.

Alpine auricula 'Victoria de Wemyss'.

This really beautiful cultivar is also known as 'Lavender Lady'. It was raised by Gordon Douglas in 1957. Walton flowers over a long period of time and holds its colours well. It is also an alpine of good constitution.

BORDER AURICULAS

The border auriculas were the archetypal cottage garden flowers once seen in many village or small-town gardens throughout the realm. It was not unusual to see the same varieties having been divided and shared growing happily in adjoining town or village gardens, as it was common practice to exchange clumps of particularly good border auriculas with one's neighbours. After many years of neglect the border auricula is now seeing a resurgence of interest, and rightly so, as the charming flowers offer a lot in way of fine garden performance, reliability and longevity.

during 1982. It can make a large plant with good flower trusses that are of a deep blue-purple that shades through to near white. It is a spectacular cultivar and a must for

collectors; a multi-award winner and deservedly so.

'Walton' is a really lovely alpine of bluish-violet shades, and is arguably the nearest to true blue found in an auricula.

Alpine auricula 'Walton'.

As mentioned previously, the border auriculas have a coating of farina on parts of the plants. This can, unfortunately, sometimes be ruined by heavy rainfall but, nonetheless, what remains is still pretty and enhances the overall impact of the plant. The flowers of the borders types are, on the whole, a little smaller than those of the alpines and are of a slightly more subdued tone, but this in no way detracts from the beauty of the flowering display. The colour range is quite extensive and includes

pink, peach, orange, white, brown, yellow, purple and more.

The borders, when grown in the garden, prefer to be out of the direct sunlight of a southerly aspect, where the fierce sun can be detrimental to the plant as a whole. Plant them in a moist but well drained soil with an organic matter content, preferably facing north or west where the gentler light will be much kinder to the plants, especially the flowers.

The quintessential English border auricula epitomizes the old-world charm of cottage gardens, and today greater interest in this type of auricula has led to the creation of more cultivars.

Border auricula 'Bellamy Pride'.

Selected border cultivars
'Bellamy Pride', *c*.1985 and bred by B. Walker, is a particularly floriferous border auricula with large white flowers, flushed with bluish pink. It has well mealed and serrated foliage. This cultivar has won awards at some shows and looks very handsome indeed when planted in a large clump.

'Blue Velvet' is a really good border auricula with a strong constitution. Sweetly scented and of a very good deep purple-blue colour, it makes a fine addition to a collection or garden border.

'Blue Wave' is an old cottage variety with a very floriferous nature. The flowers are lightly notched, creamy-centred and are held on numerous trusses. It has serrated foliage of a mid-green. 'Blue Wave' looks absolutely fabulous planted in a garden border with red-flowering bergenia.

'Broadwell Gold' is a golden yellow border auricular that was discovered by Joe Elliot thriving in a garden in Gloucestershire. Lightly crinkled petals and well-mealed foliage make this cultivar well worth seeking out.

'Chamois' has yellow frilled petals in large trusses of wash-leather yellow. This cultivar was raised by Joe Mercer.

'Dales Red' is an excellent old cultivar of vigorous growth. Its colouration is of a rich red with farina present in the centre of the flowers and it has medium-green foliage. It is well worth growing in pots under protection for showing to friends, relatives or perhaps even at a local flower show.

'Doctor Lennon's White' is quite a rare and lovely white border auricula that always creates an impact. It is very floriferous and long-flowering but, unfortunately, like many border cultivars it is seldom seen growing in gardens now.

'George Harrison' is a white-flowering border auricula that has a mid-green coloured centre. The flowers are neat, quite flat and freely produced. The foliage is well mealed and very tidy and this combines to give the whole plant an overall very neat and tidy appearance. It is not an auricula that shouts out at you but nonetheless a good one that is reliable and will please for many years.

'George Swinnerton's Leathercoat' was discovered by plant historian Ruth Duthie in a garden in Oxfordshire. It is a buff brown/pink border with serrated mealed foliage but is very difficult to come by, being a rarity now.

Border auricula 'Julie Nuttall'.

'Julie Nuttall' is a purple border with a faint pink tint to her somewhat diminutive flowers. She is nevertheless free-flowering and creates an impact, especially when planted close to a yellow border auricula such as 'Paradise Yellow'. The flowers are flat and unnotched. This cultivar offsets well and has meal-free foliage.

Border auricula 'Old Clove Red'.

In all, a lovely coloured border auricula.

'Kate Haywood' is a vigorously growing border auricula of pale yellow or creamy yellow flowers. Its light green foliage is fairly well mealed and is altogether a good border that soon makes itself at home in the garden.

'Lockyer's Gem' is an unusual border auricula as it sports spotted and striped flowers, which are of a purple hue. It is a very distinct border auricula that is a talking point, and rightly so. Worth growing if it can be obtained.

A new variety of border auricula that is causing something of a stir is the fabulous 'Lucy Locket'. This fine border has a lovely delicate scent and superbly formed flowers of pale yellow. It has begun to appear at some shows and is becoming very popular.

'McWatts Blue' sports purple-blue shaded sweet smelling flowers of fine form. It is quite floriferous and reliable with the foliage being well mealed and pert.

'Old Clove Red' is an early-flowering border with small and clove-scented velvety dark red flowers with a white mealed centre. It is a lovely and striking border that looks great planted alongside border auricula 'Paradise Yellow' or surrounded by, or next to, the blue-flowering muscari, which is a free-flowering bulbous herbaceous perennial blooming at the same time in spring.

'Old Cottage Blue' is a very lovely border auricula of lilac and blue shades. It is a very floriferous variety that produces good trusses of sweetly scented blooms.

'Old Irish Blue' is a much sought-after variety that typifies old-world charm with its soft lavender-blue flowers and delicate and subtle scent; it is worth a place in any auricula lover's garden.

'Old Red Dusty Miller' is a fine border auricula that is sometimes seen at shows. It is well regarded and sometimes puts in a stunning appearance when produced well. It has blood-coloured somewhat frayed petals and is well endowed with meal on its foliage.

A favourite border type among many growers is a variety named 'Osbourne Green'. This reliable border auricula bears frayed-edge flowers of green, cream and purple, and it flowers over a long period in the spring and early summer, and often again in the autumn months. As opposed to being flat flowered as many auriculas are, its flowers are quite deep. It is a good grower and offsets freely. It will feel very much at home in the border or alpine bed given the right conditions of good drainage and with humus incorporated into the soil. 'Osbourne Green' is reputed to have been discovered growing in a garden border in Ireland by avid gardener Mrs Wynn of Avoca in County Wicklow. She chanced upon it growing happily in the garden of a Mrs Osbourne, who is believed to have said it had been thriving there for nigh on 200 years!

'Paradise Yellow' is a bright

Border auricula 'Old Cottage Blue'.

yellow flowering border auricula with a circle of paste and mealed foliage. It is free-flowering and creates an impact when planted together with border cultivar 'Old Clove Red'.

Border auricula 'Osbourne Green'.

DOUBLE AURICULAS

If you only ever grow only one double auricula, then make sure that it is cultivar 'Fred Booley'. This purple double auricula

Border auricula 'Paradise Yellow'.

double auriculas to choose from. So how has the situation been reversed?

The double auricula has more than the usual amount of petals of the other types of auriculas. These extra petals cover the centre of the flower and can often vary in quantity. A flower with just few extra petals does not look much like a double at all, whereas a flower with, say, two extra rows would be considered to be a good double and suitable for showing, providing all the other factors are in place. Doubling occurs as a result of some plants' reproductive organs being replaced by more petals than occur on a usual auricula flower. The stamens and the pistils are not as prevalent in doubles therefore seed will not be produced in quantity, making it more difficult for these plants to reproduce naturally. This has been the determining factor for the lack of double auriculas in existence; seed production is diminished owing to the difficulty of pollination by insects and so the hand pollination technique is used in order to create the new plants.

Double auriculas have occurred naturally in the wild and were often dug up and transplanted to gardens. They were probably split and given to other gardeners to grow and admire. We have auricula breeders in the USA to thank for the prevalence of the many double cultivars now available, as much hybridizing work has gone on there, bringing us the many new varieties we enjoy today. Of course, hybridizing on

always draws comments, such as, 'What's that lovely pot plant?', or, 'That's really nice, what is it?', and sometimes, 'It's so beautiful it looks unreal.' Bred by noted auricula grower Derek Salt in 1999, this beautiful double auricula is a strong-growing and floriferous variety that is in flower throughout the spring, and is often flowering again during the late summer and early autumn. Mr Salt is a double auricula specialist who has introduced many charming and beautiful new varieties since he starting growing auriculas in 1958. Doubles have been cultivated since early times but have not been as prevalent as they are becoming today.

In his interesting book *The Auricula: The Story of a Florist's Flower* (1951), Sir Rowland Biffen, FRS, writes that the double auricula is a form that is almost lost to cultivation and that the 'surviving examples are hardly to be found outside the collections of a few enthusiastic fanciers'. He continues, 'So rare are they that most Auricula growers have never seen a specimen'.[15]

However, now we have the modern-day florists to thank for that situation being reversed. To date there are some 300 double auricula cultivars available from the nurseries specializing in auriculas. Apparently, during the period 1650 to 1750 the double auriculas were not grown on an extensive scale as '[...] the possession of a plant or two seems to have given the owners some of the prestige attached to those owning some acknowledged masterpiece of art'.[16] This seems a startling fact when nowadays we are really spoilt with so many a smaller scale is going on in Great Britain as well, by a small handful of dedicated growers.

Selected double cultivars
'Bacchante' was bred by Ken Whorton in 1998 from a red seedling × 'Susannah'. It has a sumptuous dark wine colouring and has won many prizes.

'Buttermere' was bred by Ken Whorton in 2000 from 'Sun Maiden' × 'Pegasus'. It is a fine double of a rich yellow colouring and is, rightly, increasing in popularity.

'Cadiz Bay' is a beautiful burgundy coloured double, bred by National Auricula Collection holder Les Allen in 1999. It is a very neat and photogenic auricula of very pleasing form.

'Cameo Beauty' is a creamy yellow double bred by Ken Whorton during 1994. This cultivar is a multiple award winner and rightly so as it is a real beauty.

'Chiquita' was bred by Ken Whorton from a 'Digit' × 'Susannah' cross in 1997. It is a popular double being shown regularly and winning awards. It is the colour of ginger nut sweet biscuits although is probably best described as a dark cinnamon.

'Denna Snuffer' is a pale yellow double bred by M. Smith in 1964 and named after the notable American auricula grower (Mrs Snuffer has been a double auricula hybridizer).

'Doublet' is a reliable and easy-to-grow double auricula that does not disappoint. It is a prolific offsetter so the grower should never be short of propagating material. It has attractive purple flowers and

Double auricula 'Cadiz Bay'.

was raised by Allan Hawkes in 1975.

'Doublure' is a deep red and purple double that was raised by Allan Hawkes in 1980, from 'Susannah' × 'Walton Heath'. It is a lovely full double auricula that quite captivates, although it is reputed to be a poor offsetter.

'Fred Booley' is a bright lavender-blue double, bred by Derek Salt in 1999 from 'Quatro' × 'Sarah Lodge'. This beautiful auricula is a strong-growing and floriferous variety that will grace any auricula collection.

'Funny Valentine' is a rich, deep red that is being shown regularly. It was bred by Laura Pickin in 1997 from 'Helena' × 'Corrie Files'.

'Gold Seal' was bred by Ken Ward in 1996. It is a yellow-tinged orange double auricula and an award winner at several shows. It was bred from a 'Digit' × 'Helena' cross.

'Golden Hind' is another double from Ken Whorton. It is an eye-catching gold and brown dating from 1993.

'Hoghton Gem' is from D. Cornforth c.1976. It is widely used among hybridzers as a seed parent. It is a lovely golden yellow in colour.

'Kentucky Blue' was bred by Randall Lee in 1999 and is a very good auricula blue. A lovely double auricula.

'Lincoln Imp' is a beautiful buff-coloured double bred by Derek Salt in 1996. Its availability, however, is scarce.

'Matthew Yates', by Len Bailey in 1980, is a very dark purple of dense doubling and very handsome indeed. A worthy award winner.

Another double doing well at

Double auricula 'Fred Booley'.

Tilt in 1998, from seed given by Ken Whorton. It is a multi-award winner and a must-have double for the serious collector and showperson. It has a full doubling with bright yellow colouring and, when grown well, looks a picture.

'Walton Heath' is a dark purple double of stylish good looks. It is a strong grower and was bred by Ken Gould in 1979. 'Walton Heath' is often used in auricula hybridization.

A very fine example is 'Zambia', dating from 1965 and bred by Ken Gould. It is a very eye catching double auricula of a striking dark ruby red.

the shows is 'Mipsie Miranda'. This was bred by Hazel Wood in 1980 from a Jane Myers seedling. This is a lovely lemon-coloured auricula with good doubling and neat trusses.

Double auricula 'Mipsie Miranda'.

'Mish Mish' is a semi-double auricula of yellow and biscuit brown colouring. This unusual flowered auricula was bred by Bernard Smith during 1996.

'Prima' was raised by Derek

SHOW TYPES

Green-edged auriculas

Growing edges is to many auricula growers the epitome of auricula culture; these edged beauties are considered, in some circles, to be the aristocrats of the auricula world and it is easy to see why this is so. As a result of a mutation occurring at some point in the past, the edges of the petals of this type of auricula evolved to be formed of leaf material, giving the edged auricula an illusory but very interesting texture.

To some the edged auricula in bloom appears almost too perfect – almost unreal for a living flower. Nevertheless, there is something that is fascinating and beguiling about them, especially to the newcomer.

The green-edged auriculas do not have farina present

on their flowers unlike the grey-edged and white-edged ones, which have a moderate and large amount respectively. The green colour is generally a mid-green but this varies in hue dependent on the cultivar.

All edged auriculas have a tube of a gold colour holding the reproductive organs. This is surrounded by a circle of paste, which is also known as the eye; this should be white in colour and is the farina-covered disc. Then comes the body colour, also known as the ground colour; this should be black and radiate evenly into the edge. Ideally there should be no 'flashing', that, is the body colour should not have streaks that extend into the edge colour. Body colours other than black are not acceptable and those flowers showing a variation are known as fancy auriculas. The above gives you some indication of what is required to grow an acceptable green-edged auricula.

Roland Biffen said that the name of the green-edge defines its class sufficiently. He also says that the green coloration is of various shades, somewhere between the green of grass and the green of the foliage of the yew tree. He goes on to say that, hypothetically, the green should extend to the extreme margin of the corolla, and that this is mainly the case but there are exceptions in newer varieties. Some of these modern sorts, he wrote, '[...]have small white areas of meal on the corolla edge. If it is not too evident a

Double auricula 'Mish Mish'.

judge will often overlook their presence, however, some of the Lancashire florists had no hesitation in classing these plants as China-edge'.[17]

This tangible essence of auricula culture is indicative of how our forebears viewed and judged auriculas. Today, the physical characteristics of the edged auricula at flower shows should conform to an exacting

Double auricula 'Walton Heath'.

Green edge auricula 'Bob Lancashire'.

Victory' was one of the first green-edged auriculas recorded as growing in 1746 and by all accounts was received with great acclaim on its introduction and was a sure-fire winner at the shows of that time. Today the green edges are still, to many growers, the Rolls Royce of auriculas.

Selected green-edged cultivars

'Beechen Green' was bred by L.E. Wigley during 1970. It is a good green show edge of excellent flowering performance. The flowers, of a bright green, tend to be rather on the small side. It has a light dusting of meal on medium green foliage. This cultivar is quite a reliable offsetter.

standard, and this is laid out in the exhibition requirements.

The edges were the auricula of preference during the eighteenth and nineteenth centuries. There were many varieties, holding such enigmatic names as 'Rule Arbiter', 'Pollitt's Ruler of England' and 'Lightbody's Star of Bethlehem' – all green edges. Cultivar 'Taylor's

'Bob Lancashire' is a fine green-edged cultivar and was bred by Jack Wemyss-Cooke, using 'Chloë' × 'Geldersome Green' in 1984. It is considered an easy plant to grow and rewards the grower with producing a good quantity of offsets.

'Bucks Green' is a very reliable green edge that produces fine trusses of well-formed pips. It is a good offsetter that makes a fine addition to any grower's, particularly a novice's, collection. The foliage matches the green of the edge very well.

'Chloë' was originally raised by the late Fred Buckley of Macclesfield in 1957 and was first seen on the show benches in 1967. The following year it won a Premier Award. 'Chloë' could be regarded as a paradigm among green

Green edge auricula 'Bucks Green'.

edges; it has been shown on very many occasions since its introduction as it has set standards by which others are judged.

'Figaro' is a fine green-edged show auricula that is the result of a 'Chloë' × 'Haffner' cross. It was bred by David Hadfield during 1985.

'Fleminghouse' is another superb green-edge of great form and is considered as one of the, if not *the*, very best edge auriculas in circulation. It has won numerous top awards and it is no wonder. It is seen in some circles to be the main competitor to 'Chloë'. 'Fleminghouse' was bred by J. Stant in 1967.

'Jupiter' was bred by David Hadfield in 1976 from a 'Fleminghouse' and a seedling. It is a pale green colour and has won at the shows.

'Marmion' is an older green edge, *c.*1900, from the House of Douglas. It is quite a scarce green edge now and is seldom seen on the plant lists, but is well worth growing if you can find it.

'Orb' was bred by Dr D. Duthie by a 'James Stockhill' × 'Blisterine' cross in 1970. A little farina is occasionally present on the petals. 'Orb' is capable of producing fine specimens but is inclined to be rather erratic in performance. Nevertheless, it is worth adding to a collection.

'Paris' was raised by David Hadfield in 1978 and was awarded the coveted Corsar Cup in 1981.

'Prague', which was bred by David Hadfield from a 'Chloë' × 'Fleminghouse' cross in 1976,

Green edge auricula 'Serenity'.

is one of the best show greens in cultivation. It is a strong grower of good form but is apt to produce pips of varying sizes and shapes. When grown well it displays good flowering performance and style.

'Prosperine' was bred by Ken Whorton from a cross of 'Fleminghouse' × 'Roberto'. It was first shown in 2001 and won seedling classes at the Uplands and Knowle Auricula Shows.

'Sappho', named after the ancient Greek poet, was first bred by David Hadfield from 'Roberto'. It is considered in showing circles to be a nice and neat green edge with a good future.

'Serenity' is a 1957-bred green edge by Jack Ballard. It is regarded as a reliable grower and ideal for the novice grower as it produces offsets fairly well.

'Tamino' was bred by David Hadfield from 'Chloë' × 'Jupiter'. 'Tamino' is becoming very popular with exhibitors and in some circles is seen as a possible rival to 'Prague'.

'Tinkerbell' was introduced in 1932 by C. Cookson and was *the* green edge to grow and show for many years during the 1960s. It was often a winner when it was exhibited but enjoys only patchy success today. 'Tinkerbell' has been a difficult green edge to grow well and at one stage was almost lost to cultivation. Micro-propagation has saved it and it is now becoming more readily available from auricula nurseries again.

'Warwick' was bred by Peter Ward in 1976 using 'Walhampton' × 'Teem'. It is a really good grey/white edge but tends to be a little late flowering. It has moderately

Green edge 'Tinkerbell'.

mealed and deeply serrated leaves of good form. It has won many prizes and is regarded as a stalwart amongst white edges.

Grey-edged and white-edged auriculas

The difference between the green-edged and the grey-edged auriculas is that the latter have only a light sprinkling of farina present, not only on the foliage but, more importantly, on the flowers. A grey-edged auricula in full bloom is a wonderful sight. To me the sight of a well-grown grey-edged auricula epitomizes all that is best in auricula floristry. The blend of the black body colour and green edge sprinkled with a light dusting of white farina, making the petal appear grey, together with the bright golden tube, could be described as floral perfection.

The distinction between the grey edges and the white edges is the intensity of the meal present on the petals. Whereas grey edges often have varying degrees of attached meal, the sheer intensity of meal to completely mask the green colouration of the petal gives us the white edges.

Selected grey-edged cultivars
'Ben Wyves' is generally a strong-growing grey-edged auricula that produces good strong trusses. It is a reliable plant that offsets fairly well.

'Clare' was bred by Peter Ward in 1980 by crossing 'Walhampton' × 'Helena'. It is a fine example of a show-winning grey-edged auricula. 'Clare' displays, as do some other grey-edged auriculas, a silver-coloured margin to the edge of the petals that further enhance

the exquisite beauty of these grey-edge auriculas.

'Gavin Ward' was bred by Peter Ward during 1976 from a 'Walhampton' × 'Teem' cross. This grey edge was named after his son. It is a good and reliable grower but unfortunately is not a good offsetter so it is a fairly scarce plant. The photograph shown here of a single pip illustrates how exquisite a well-grown edged auricula can be. Gavin Ward is a multiple award winner.

'Grey Hawk' was bred by David Hadfield in 1988 from a 'Hawkwood' and an unnamed fancy cross. It is a very good show variety but to its detriment can be a slow auricula to mature. Nevertheless, it is a very good grey edge and well worth seeking out.

'Iago' is another good grey-edged auricula and was bred by David Hadfield in 1988 from 'Grey Friar' × 'Stephen'.

'Lovebird' is a grey-edge show auricula raised by James Douglas in 1908. It is regarded as a reliable old variety of neat and tidy serrated mealy foliage. It has rather small pips but, nevertheless, they are neat and attractive. This cultivar is a multi-award winning variety that is still very popular today.

'Margaret Martin' was bred by A.J. Martin from a 'Lovebird' × 'Teem' cross during 1973. When it made its debut in 1974 it won the Corsar Cup, among other prizes. It went on to win numerous other awards and is still highly regarded but seen by some as rather unreliable.

'Silverways' is a striking grey-edged show auricula that is well worth having in any collection. It is a reliable cultivar and a good offsetter.

'Snowy Owl', raised in 1986, is a grey-edged or white-edged auricula. It is rather similar to 'Teem'.

'Teem' is a very fine variety, bred in 1959 by T. Meek. It is a well-used pollen parent for many other grey edges and won the Corsar Cup on its first appearance in Manchester. It is a robust, strong growing and good offsetting grey-edged auricula of great popularity.

Selected white-edged cultivars

'Brookfield' is a reliable white-edged auricula cultivar that was bred by Peter Ward. This auricula came from a 'Walhampton' × 'Teem 2' cross in 1979. It is a free-flowering white edge but difficult to get to a good showing standard. Nevertheless, it is well worth growing and is readily available from many auricula nurseries.

'Colbury' is a beautiful cultivar that dates back to 1955. It was bred by the renowned auricula expert C.G. Haysom and is still performing well today. This cultivar epitomizes the white-edged auricula type. It was named after the charming Hampshire village of Colbury.

'C.G. Haysom' was raised by R. Loake in 1962 and has a dark body with a good white edge. It is an excellent, reliable and popular plant and worthy of a place in a collection of grey edges. Mr C.G. Haysom was a notable auricula hybridizer

Grey edge auricula 'Silverways'.

who introduced many edged cultivars, particularly the grey edges.

'Jorvik' was raised by Tim Coop in 2001/2002 and was first shown at Cheadle in 2003 where it gained a first prize. It takes its name from the Viking for York, which was the Scandinavian seat of power in these isles during the ninth and tenth centuries.

Grey edge auricula 'Gavin Ward'.

White edge auricula 'Brookfield'.

'Maggie' dates from 1966 when it was introduced by A. Hawkes. It is a fairly diminutive pretty flower but nonetheless very pleasing to look at.

White edge auricula 'Colbury'.

'Ptarmigan' bred by Tim Coop is a well-named auricula sharing the same colouration as the game bird. It is not readily available at present but hopefully will become more widespread in the not-too-distant future.

'Sharman's Cross' was raised by Peter Ward in 1976. It is a result of a 'Walhampton' × 'Teem' cross. It is a good white edge but is purported to be erratic in performance. It was named after an area of Birmingham.

'Walhampton' is a very good cultivar bred by C.G. Haysom in 1946. It has been used as a parent plant in hybridizing and is a very good white edge in its own right for showing.

'Warwick' was bred by Peter Ward in 1976 using 'Walhampton' × 'Teem'. It has a very white edge but tends to be a little late flowering. It has moderately mealed and deeply serrated leaves of good form. It has won many prizes and is regarded as a stalwart amongst green edges.

'White Ensign' is a lovely old white-edge Douglas variety raised in 1950. It is an excellent white-edged auricula with serrated and well-mealed foliage and is very worthy of being placed in a collection. It offsets fairly freely and, as such, is a good white edge for the beginner.

Fancy auriculas

Could the fancy auricula be described as the Cinderella of the auricula world? This question arises because the definition of a fancy auricula is an edged auricula that does not have a black ground colour (or body colour; that is, the colour ring adjoining the ring of paste). The colours may be yellow, red, maroon, purple, pink or brown. These ground colours

often flash out far into the edge colour of grey, white or green. Some growers consider these plants to be inferior to the black-bodied plants and will not entertain them but, on the other hand, many of these fancies do have a lovely appearance and some are quite striking and very collectable.

Rowland Biffen, in his 1951 book, said that the fancies were not and have never been regarded with much significance, but as there was an interest in this type of auricula mention must be made of them. He goes on to say that there were two types that were representative of the category. The first was a green kind that sees the colour extending to the paste with tiny flecks of golden yellow at the points of junction with the petals. The other, which he says was often listed as a yellow ground fancy, had a bright buttercup yellow in the region occupied by the body colour in the edge group, and the tips of the petals, which may be mealed, were green.[18]

By contrast, today there are many varieties of fancies that are readily available and they enjoy a good and increasing popularity, and deservedly so. Renowned auricula grower James Douglas has raised many new fancy auriculas, as have breeders Tim Coop and James Douglas.

Selected fancy cultivars
'Astolat' was raised by R.W. Hecker in 1971 and has colours of green, light red and mauve. It is a good fancy for the beginner as it offsets well

White edge auricula 'Jorvik'.

and is a prolific grower. A well-grown plant of 'Astolat' is an auricula well worth seeing. It is named after the legendary city of Astolat in Arthurian tales.

'Colonel Champneys' is an

old cultivar with a military-sounding name. It was bred in 1867 by a Mr W.Turner. It is a light purple and maroon with a green edge and a good circle of paste. It has certainly stood the

White edge auricula 'Maggie'.

Fancy auricula 'Idmiston'.

test of time and is still offered by some nurseries today.

'Daffie Green' is a purple-bodied fancy with a narrow green edge that is sometimes mealed on the tips. It is a diminutive and neat plant, one which offsets freely giving plenty of material for the owner.

'Fleet Street' is a vibrantly coloured fancy auricula bred by

Fancy auricula 'Laverock'.

Henry Pugh in 2002. It is from a cross between 'Marion Tiger' and a red self seedling from 'Red Admiral'. This is a newer cultivar that will surely have a good future with the breeders.

'Grey Monarch' was bred by James Douglas in 1959. It is a yellow and grey coloured fancy of good reliability and form; it offsets freely so is a good one for the novice but is also worth showing: a good all-rounder.

'Hawkwood' has a dark red body with a grey edge and was bred by James Douglas in 1970. It offsets freely and is a reliable fancy auricula of good form.

'Hinton Fields' is a very fine fancy auricula of bright yellow with a green edge. A 'Spring Meadows' natural cross which was raised by A.J. Martin in 1967 and shown in the same year.

'Idmiston', raised by Gordon Douglas, is a reliable fancy auricula of green and red colouring that always pleases. It is easy to grow, offsets reasonably and is fairly vigorous in growth, thereby making it a good variety for the beginner or collector.

'Laverock' was raised by Gordon Douglas in 1983. It is a green and red seedling from 'Rolts'; it is a strong grower that offsets fairly readily and therefore is another good one for the novice.

'Minley', which was raised by Gordon Douglas in 1982, has lovely magenta and green flowers held above serrated foliage. It is an easy fancy to grow, and is a very free offsetter.

'Portree' was bred in 1984 is

a 'Rolts' × 'Rajah' cross. It is a vigorous grower that is reliable and a fairly good offsetter.

'Rajah', bred in the 1950s by James Douglas, is an easy-to-grow fancy of good reliability for general use but is apparently difficult to bring into good enough form for show purposes. It is a very distinctive auricula with red and olive-green flowers.

'Spring Meadow' is a green-edge fancy auricula, c.1957, which has a bright yellow body and a bright white circle of paste. It is a cultivar of good constitution and is very reliable. It always flowers well and is a must-have in any collection.

'Star Wars' is proving to be a very popular fancy. It was bred by Tim Coop using a pin-eyed purple seedling with a grey edge. It is a very handsome auricula, instantly recognizable and photogenic.

Self auriculas

There has been a rise and fall in the popularity of self auriculas since they first appeared on the floristry scene. Around the turn of the twentieth century there were relatively few self auriculas available, but modern means of propagation have greatly increased the number prevalent today. These lovely show auriculas have a uniform body colour extending from the circle of paste to the outer margin of the flower edge, and this is the most straightforward and obvious method of identification for auricula novices. Evident by definition, the term self as an adjective means self-coloured: having the same colour all over.

Fancy auricula 'Spring Meadow'.

The self auriculas colours are yellow, blue (purple), red and very deep red (almost black). Other colours are placed in the 'any other colour' category. These include: brown, mushroom, orange, pink, pink hues, lavender and lilac. The colours of the selfs are particularly bright and they have the beauty of simplicity with jewel-like flower colours. When meal is present on the foliage there is not a lot to beat the selfs for their sheer simplicity and brilliance.

Selected self cultivars

'Alice Haysom' is a red show self bred by C.G. Haysom in 1935. It is an auricula of a deep red colour and has well-farinated foliage adding to the fine looks of this show cultivar.

'April Moon' is a good show variety with large pips. It was bred by Tim Coop in 1988 from a 'Moonglow' × 'Helen' cross. With its very lovely pale yellow flowers 'April Moon' is often seen on the show benches and rightly so as it is a good self auricula with very fine looks.

'Atlantic' was bred by P. Ward during 1993 and is a good dark blue that tends to be an early flowerer and gives a nice display in very early spring.

'Barbarella' was bred by Peter Ward in 1980 using 'Pat' × 'Rosalind' × 'Mikado'. It is proving to be an excellent show variety and is one of the very best dark selfs. It is so dark as to appear almost black, which is a characteristic of quite a few of the darker red selfs. It is a robust auricula and trouble-free cultivar.

'Bilton' is a fine yellow self, bred by Derek Telford in 1970. It has handsome well-mealed, lightly serrated and quite rounded foliage.

Self auricula 'April Moon'.

'Cheyenne', which was bred in 1971, is a result of a 'Pat' × HMR1 ('Hall Mikado' × 'Rosalind') cross. It was bred by P. Ward and is one of the darker reds but by no means is it as dark red as 'Mikado'.

'Corn Time' is a popular yellow self that was bred by Tim Coop in 1988 from a cross between cultivars 'Moonglow' × 'Helen' and is proving a winner at the shows.

'Cortina' is named after the popular Ford saloon car of the 1960s to 1980s. This stunning red self was bred by Derek Telford in 1983 and is a particularly beautiful show auricula that always cuts a dash!

'Eventide' is a very pleasant blue self that was bred by renowned auricula grower Derek Telford. The colour is almost purple in appearance in certain light. This plant is reliable and always flowers well.

'Fanny Meerbeck' is an old cultivar that was bred by Ben Simonite in 1898, and it is still going strong today. It is a good grower and produces clear red flowers. It has lovely heavily mealed foliage, which is nicely serrated.

'Geronimo' was bred by Peter Ward in 1971. It is a good red self of golden farina and has the same breeding as 'Cheyenne' and 'Chiricahua'.

'Helen' is a good yellow self for the novice grower, as it is a reliable cultivar that produces many offsets and numerous pips. The mature leaves can be strap-like and well covered with meal. Occasionally, during the winter

Self auricula 'Alice Haysom'.

months the meal will change to a lovely gold colouration. It was produced by Tim Coop of Harrogate in 1981 and is becoming used frequently as a pollen parent.

Self auricula 'Bilton'.

'Joel' is an easy-to-grow and very popular blue self. It was bred by Cynthia Bach in 1952 from cultivar 'Blue Jean'. 'Joel' appears quite often in nursery stock lists and on the Internet.

Self auricula 'Cortina'.

'Limelight' is a great variety, which was bred by Tim Coop in 1988 from a 'Moonglow' × 'Moneymoon' cross. It is a little lighter in colour than 'Moonglow' and falls into the 'any other colour' category. It often appears on the show benches.

'Margaret Thatcher' was bred by Jack Wemyss-Cooke in 1988. A true blue lady! This is a reliable self that always gives a fine performance.

'Mikado', bred in 1906 by W. Smith, has deservedly been a multi-prize winner over the years. It is a very dark-flowered cultivar of the highest order and is still winning first prizes in the dark self class – it is probably the best cultivar in its rather small class. It has very distinctive serrated leaves that are meal-free, long and hang over the flower pots in which it is grown. The pips are of a very dark red, appearing almost black depending on the viewing aspect. A popular variety.

'Moonglow', bred by David Hadfield in 1975, is placed in the 'any other colour' category. The colour is hard to define, suffice to say that the parentage is of 'Leeside Yellow' × 'Ower'. It could be described as a pale lemon/grey wash. It is a regular on the show bench and is often used in hybridizing.

'Neat and Tidy' does what it says. It is a lovely and trouble-free dark show self, sometimes quite diminutive, bred by Doctor Newton in 1955. It is certainly one for the collection.

'Oakes Blue' is still regarded as one of the best blue selfs. It was bred by Derek Telford, in 1974, and is a rich deep purple. Its parentage is of cultivars 'Stella' × 'Everest Blue'.

'Old Gold' is another of the old cultivars that was bred by J. Douglas in 1920. It is not one that is easy to source now but it is still around.

Among the many fine blue self auriculas is 'Remus', bred by W.R. Hecker in the 1960s. It is a prolific flowerer that has to

Self auricula 'Eventide'.

be thinned in order to show an acceptable truss. Likewise the offsets require to be thinned out to show a good plant. It is another ideal self auricula for the novice grower. It is dark blue in colour.

'Renata' is a self of fairly vigorous growth that produces good, clear blue flowers. It has nice but lightly mealed foliage, and was bred by W. Hecker in 1970.

'Sharon Louise' is an outstanding yellow self that was bred by Ken Bowser in 1991 from a 'Brompton' × 'Upton Belle' cross. It is a relatively late-flowering variety of beautiful form.

'Sheila' was bred by Alan Hawkes during 1961. She is a fine pale to mid-yellow self depending on the light available, but looks almost gold during the late spring sunshine. It is a very fine self auricula.

'Simply Red' is a fine self named after the popular music group. This reliable show auricula, which was bred by Tim Coop, always gives a star performance.

'Tom Boy', produced by Tim Coop in 1984, is a very good show variety that is from a 'Moonglow' × 'Helen' cross.

'Trudy' is a red show self of a dark hue. It was bred by Derek Telford in 1980. It has nicely mealed foliage and is altogether a very neat self that behaves well.

Striped auriculas

The striped auriculas have had a somewhat chequered history. They were very popular during the seventeenth century and

Self auricula 'Fanny Meerbeck'.

continued to be avidly grown through to the late eighteenth century. After this time they all but disappeared from the florists' scene, the reasons why one cannot tell, but thankfully their re-emergence is as a result of sterling work by a few dedicated breeders. John Rea (d. 1681), nurseryman and florist of Kinlet, Shropshire, had several striped auriculas that

Self auricula 'Helen'.

Self auricula 'Neat and Tidy'.

which reigned supreme, or whether it was a result of the dissatisfaction with the few varieties of striped auriculas available, and difficulties in propagation, is a moot point. Whatever the reason, there was a void in the florists' repertoire that would not start to be filled again until the 1960s when, with the determination of a few hybridizers, new varieties began to appear on the scene.

It was renowned auricula specialist Allan Hawkes who used an auricula that showed a tendency to striping, which was donated to him by Dr Cecil Jones of Llanelli, and embarked on a breeding programme to try and resurrect the type. Results were patchy at first but gradually new varieties of merit began to be produced.

were eventually passed onto his son-in-law the Reverend Gilbert, an avid auricula florist.

By the middle of the eighteenth century stripes were still in evidence, as shown by noted garden illustrators of the day, but after this time their presence seems to have all but disappeared. Whether it was because of the great interest in the edged auricula,

Selected striped cultivars

'Arundel Stripe' was bred by Ray Downard during 1986. It has proved to be a very popular striped auricula, which is sweetly scented, being yellow with heavy red and maroon striping, and it has a white centre. It is an easy-to-grow auricula that offsets freely and, as such, is a good auricula for the novice grower.

'Blackpool Rock' was bred by Allan Guest in 1988 from 'Error' × 'Singer Stripe'. It is a charming pink and pale-yellow stripe with the pink colour being predominant.

'Blush Baby' is a red and grey striped auricular that offsets freely. It is another good one for the beginner and is becoming popular at the shows.

Self auricula 'Simply Red'.

Self auricula 'Sheila'.

Self auricula 'Trudy'.

'Crinoline' is a lovely striped auricula of lavender and green and was raised by Tim Coop.

'Karen Cordrey' is a neat and tidy striped auricula of black and white flowers, sometimes appearing more like a fancy.

'Königin de Nacht' is a heavily mealed striped auricula bred by Allan Guest in 1998. It is not black striped, as may be thought at first glance, but is actually deep purple over white. It is named after the character 'Queen of the Night' from Mozart's *Magic Flute* opera of 1791. It is a reliable cultivar that offsets freely.

Another striped auricula of great interest and increasing popularity is the lovely cultivar 'Lord Saye and Sele'. It has yellow and green stripes, terracotta blotches and a white centre. It was first raised by Allan Hawkes during 1987. It is now being grown and offered by most of the auricula nurseries.

'May Tiger' has grey stripes over a maroon ground; these old-fashioned colours blend well together. It is a very smart auricula that was first raised by A. Hawkes in 1986.

'Raleigh Stripe' is a bright striped auricula, bred by A. Guest in 1979, of a vivid red over a taupe ground cover. This plant is very striking and is certainly one for the collection.

'Rover Stripe' was introduced by Allan Hawkes in 1975. It has deep red stripes on top of grey. It is a nicely mealed and very good-looking striped auricula.

'Tay Tiger' is a velvety red and light green /grey striped auricula of charm. It also has nicely mealed foliage and good form. It offsets quite well and is another good one for the novice.

Striped auricula 'Königin de Nacht'.

Striped auricula 'Lord Saye and Sele'.

Alpine auricula 'Fairy'.

3 How to Grow Auriculas

The following is a monthly guide to what should be done to look after auriculas throughout the year.

JANUARY

During the winter there is really not a lot to do to your auricula collection other than to keep a close eye on your plants. They must be kept very much on the dry side, but not to the point of wilt.

Auriculas growing in clay pots will naturally stay drier than those grown in plastic plant pots, with clay being permeable and the plastic not. You may be lucky enough to obtain some Victorian-era 'Long Tom' clay pots. It is traditional practice to place a shard or shards of broken pieces of clay pot into the bottom of your pot before adding compost and the auricula plant. The shards will sit over the drainage hole, which is often quite large in the Victorian Long Tom, and will prevent worms, vine weevil and other crawling insects from entering the pots, and disturbing and eating the roots of your prized auriculas. Break up pieces of broken pots now to fit the holes for use at potting time.

Only water auriculas during this winter period if really necessary. The tell-tale sign as to when water is required will be flaccid leaves and the surface of the compost having shrunk away from the edge of the pots. Being of an alpine origin, auriculas will naturally prefer growing conditions much as they would be in their native habitat. The conditions that these plants endure in their natural habitat cannot be replicated exactly in our gardens and greenhouses but by giving auriculas as much fresh air as possible, and keeping them on the dry side during the winter months, they should reward the grower with wonderful displays from March to May, and often a little longer. When watering, avoid getting water onto the foliage and especially the crown of the plants. Left for a night wet, the leaves will quickly turn yellow and rot will set into the crowns of the plants.

Look over the plants regularly and remove yellow or brown/grey leaves with a scalpel or very sharp scissors. This process, along with copious quantities of fresh air, should keep any fungal disease away.

Keep their accommodation well ventilated at all times and do not worry about frost; auriculas are hardy plants and must not be coddled! A greenhouse with all vents controlled by automatic ventilators and the door left open is ideal housing for auriculas throughout winter and spring. If you are growing them in cold frames keep the glass frames (lights) on to protect against rain but try and prop them open for ventilation ensuring, if possible, that rain does not infiltrate the frames.

FEBRUARY

Arguably it is February that is the most exciting time of the year for auricula growers. The plants will begin stirring this month by slowly unfolding fresh foliage. As the days gradually lengthen the auriculas will continue to emerge from their near dormancy at a faster rate as the month progresses. Careful watering should be given as necessary. As new growth accelerates so more water will be required, but beware, as damage may be done by excessive watering, especially if the weather becomes damp and cold again and adequate ventilation is not given. If watering is required, either stand the pots in a tray of water for a few minutes or water very carefully from the top.

As in January, keep the auriculas tidy by removing decaying or dead leaves. Do not attempt to pull dead leaves away without supporting the main body of the auricula with your other hand. Damage can be inflicted all too easily by not taking care. If leaf removal is done carelessly infection may enter through the ragged ends of the dead leaves still partially attached to the plant, or through the scar that is left. It is good practice to dust the area of the plant with flowers of sulphur after leaf removal. This powder will prevent infection.

Scrape away any loose material from the top surface of the pot and renew with a little fresh compost. Offsets that may mar the overall appearance of your plants may be rubbed out by your fingers, or removed and rooted in free-draining compost. Careful liquid fertilizing may begin now or left a week or so, to encourage healthy growth.

Sow auricula seed from early in the month in pots, trays or pans. Cover the seed only very lightly with sieved compost or vermiculite and do not use any artificial heat at all. Cover the containers in polystyrene or glass sheets.

MARCH

The days continue to lengthen and by the end of the month it is light at around 07.30 and darkness falls around 18.30; as new growth continues to gather pace your auriculas will require more water. If you have not already done so, start to feed them now by adding liquid fertilizer. There are numerous brands of high-ratio potash liquid fertilizer on the market. They are sold generally as tomato fertilizer with NPK ratios of, for example, 5:2.5:10 or 16:4:27; use at a half-strength dilution rate for the former fertilizer and at a quarter strength for the latter.

Do not allow your auriculas to dry out as to do so will cause a check in bud formation and so result in poorer flowering.

Some alpine and self auriculas will be starting to get ready to flower now and any that have colour showing in their buds should continue be fertilized at full or half-rate dilution. Beware that too much fertilizer may spoil flowering by the production of floppy stems and over-large pips.

Ensure that good shading of the greenhouse or frames is in place. This is the best time to apply Liquid Coolglass™ if that is your preferred method. The sun, when it makes an appearance, can be quite fierce through the glass and will dry out the auriculas rapidly.

If you are going to show your auriculas then staking them with plastic-coated wire or thin split canes may now be necessary for those cultivars that do not have strong stems. Also keep your auriculas clean by washing the foliage carefully with moistened cotton wool if dirty and be sure to remember to remove any dead leaves hidden by the foliage above.

APRIL/MAY

Now it is all happening! Auricula foliage continues to grow and multiply and the flower stalks of the early flowerers are extending ever upwards. Many alpines and selfs will be showing their vibrant colours at this time from the opening of swollen buds at the top of the flower stalks, which will be at their optimum height now. Smell the air, especially on first entering the greenhouse, and breathe in the delicate fragrance permeating

the atmosphere. Delightful! Make a note of those varieties displaying characteristics that you feel will make good attributes to carry over to newly raised crosses. Start to cross-pollinate your selected auriculas, ensuring you clearly label those that you do.

Beware of sudden and unexpected late sharp frosts. To protect your plants place sheets of newspapers over the top of split canes placed strategically in some of the auricula pots. Close the greenhouse door overnight if the frost is accompanied by fog. Shut the vents or frame lights and open them up again first thing in the morning.

Most of the alpines and selfs will be free-flowering now, but the doubles and edges are generally a little later to start flowering, although there are often variations from year to year.

Pick out your finest specimens and try your luck at the shows. Most importantly, enjoy your auriculas. Take some into your house for the family to enjoy and allow them to forgive you for spending so much time in the greenhouse!

JUNE

Post-flowering there are plenty of tasks to do to ensure you achieve even better results next spring. Some of your auriculas will naturally begin to slow down their growth now. Remove unwanted dead flower stalks by cutting halfway down the footstalks with scissors or a scalpel. Do not cut right down to the base of the plants but let the stalks wither naturally.

Collect ripened seed from seed heads when ready. Put the gathered seed in aluminium foil folds in the bottom of your refrigerator, and leave them there until seed-sowing time.

Pot on rooted offsets into small pots – auriculas do not like to be over-potted, so use the smallest pots suitable for the root volume. Take more offsets to increase your stock, and also pot on those auriculas requiring a larger-sized pot up to a maximum of a 3½in (90mm) diameter pot. At this time trim away with scissors any poor looking roots before potting. It is best to re-pot auriculas now, before the hottest part of the year, or leave this operation until September, when the weather is cooler.

Plants that have reached their third year in their final pots should have their roots washed free of compost, trimmed with scissors as necessary, and the bottom part of the carrots cut away if there is sign of disease, rot or if they look pitted. Dust the wound with flowers of sulphur before potting them again in fresh compost. This method, which has been used since very early times of auricula culture, will reinvigorate older plants.

It is good practice to water your auriculas using a solution of Provado®. This liquid insecticide will prevent the pernicious insect vine weevil (*Otiorhynchus sulcatus*) from playing havoc with your prized specimens.

JULY/AUGUST

Provide maximum ventilation to cold frames and greenhouses at this time. Automatic roof vents are temperature sensitive and will probably be open before you make your early morning greenhouse visit. If your greenhouse has them, side ventilators should remain open as often as possible.

Regularly dampen the benches and floors with water to try and keep the temperatures down and, most importantly, to deter red spider mite (*Tetranychus urticae*). This microscopic insect is a sap-sucker and by definition will draw out the moisture from auricula foliage; an infestation will weaken the auricula constitution and render plants unsightly. Owing to its minute size the red spider mite it is not easily seen, even by the most eagle-eyed grower, but what will readily be noticed will be the mottling and webbing effect on auricula leaves. The red spider mite loves a hot and dry atmosphere and breeds rapidly, so immediate action will be necessary. Proprietary insecticides containing the chemical ingredient bifenthrin will control this most pernicious of pests.

In general, maintain a lookout for insects and spray with appropriate garden insecticides if necessary, but do remove what you can manually. Keep your auriculas moist by careful watering and continue to gather seed. The floor of the greenhouse is often cooler than the benches or stages and it may be a good idea to move what you can to the floor if there is a spell of very hot weather.

SEPTEMBER

At this time of the year your auriculas should be ready for their winter dormancy, but there is sometimes a surge of new growth in late summer and early autumn and some auriculas will throw up new flowers. I tend to enjoy these late blooms by bringing these plants into my home to appreciate the late display. Remember that by coming into a home the compost will dry out quicker owing to the warmer atmosphere. To this end, stand the plants in pot-plant saucers and pour water into these if the auriculas require watering.

Water as necessary but be careful not to over-water as cold weather is just around the corner and your auriculas will not take kindly to being saturated at this cooler time of the year. Ensure all re-potting and potting on is completed by the end of the month to allow the roots to settle in and anchor themselves; a little new growth will assure you that this is happening.

Auriculas that have spent the summer months in cold frames should be moved back into the cold and unheated greenhouse at the end of the month. This will enable you to oversee the welfare of the plants more easily.

Ensure there are no insects in the compost of the plants,

but this should not be a problem if crocks have been placed in the bottom of the pots at potting time. To check, invert the pots, placing your fingers over the top of the compost surface, and tap the rim of the pots on a hard surface, usually the edge of a potting bench. This should enable the pot to slide off easily for you to inspect the soil. Any nasties need to be removed and disposed of elsewhere. Inspect the compost thoroughly. Some pests are very adept at entering the drainage holes if they are not protected.

Now is a good time of the year to treat the auricula plants against vine weevil for a second time. Use Provado®, which is readily available at garden centres, at the manufacturer's recommended rates of use.

More offsets may now be taken, and you should place them in moist but not too wet compost in small pots. I use 2½in (65mm) pots for this purpose, or 3in (75mm) pots for three or more offsets, and set them around the pot's edge.

Liquid Coolglass™ shading may be removed from the greenhouse now. Use a dry cloth and just wipe it away on a dry day. Removal will admit maximum light as we move into the winter months. I allow nature to do this for me, as by the end of the month the autumn rains have washed off most of the Coolglass from the roof of the greenhouses leaving just the sides still shaded, albeit not quite so heavily.

Alpine auricula 'Avril'. (Photo: Drointon Nurseries)

OCTOBER/NOVEMBER AND DECEMBER

We have reached the time of year when your auriculas are probably looking very jaded. Leaves die off and they will sometimes shrink back to a central bud or carrot. During mild winters, however, the auricula foliage will not die down as it would during a traditional cold winter. This situation means that auricula growers have to be extra vigilant by removing decaying and dead leaves regularly. The development of mould (botrytis) in these conditions is quite likely. This will be noticed by a whitish-grey fluff material on the lower footstalks of the plants if they have been affected. If ignored it will spread and kill your plants. Proprietary fungicides are available but it is preferable to practise cultural control, by adequate ventilation, vigilance and judicious watering regimes.

Avoid having auricula plants on staging that can be rained on by being close to the greenhouse door, directly beneath the roof vents or very close to side ventilation. Auriculas require to be watered once in every three weeks throughout the winter months. However this is very much dependent on the compost composition, type of flower pot (whether plastic or clay), winter temperatures and plant growth. Some auriculas, especially the alpines, will continue to grow a little during mild spells of weather. Allow plenty of space between the pots on the staging to encourage unrestricted air circulation.

And so we are back to where we started. Another January, and the cycle begins once more.

Seasons of the Northern Hemisphere

23 March	Spring starts	VE (vernal equinox)
20/21 June	Summer starts	SS (summer starts)
22/23 September	Autumn starts	AE (autumnal equinox)
21/22 December	Winter starts	WS (winter starts)

The seasons for the southern hemisphere are the opposite of those for the northern hemisphere:

September to December = Spring
December to March = Summer
March to June = Autumn (fall)
June to September = Winter

COMPOSTS

Composts of old

Historically an array of dubious materials has been used for auricula composts; materials such as bullocks' blood, blacke mold (?), willow earth, rotten cow dung and night dung! Matthew Kenney, a mid-eighteenth century gardener, and reportedly one of the most successful and eminent growers of auriculas in his day, won numerous prizes for his auriculas using a compost made from stable loam of a sandy nature, which he 'sweetened' by constant turning.

He mixed this with sheep dung and hay litter, which was well rotted; this was mixed and turned regularly and was not used for at least twelve to eighteen months, by which time the mixture had the appearance of leaf mould or fine vegetable mould. Occasionally he incorporated a small portion of cow dung and a little coarse sand. This was Kenney's general mix for potting auriculas but for top-dressing his plants, which he did twice each year, he used stronger and more astonishing compost. To the loam and sheep dung he added a blend of poultry dung bound together with sheeps' blood. Kenney had an agreement with slaughterers and farmers in Finchley, London, to reserve for him the sheeps' blood as it became available.

Old-Fashioned Auricula Compost

A dubious uricula compost mix of yesteryear would include the following, as presented by Thomas Hogg in 1839:

- ⅓ Fresh yellow loam, or maiden mould
- ⅓ Cow dung, well rotten,
- ⅓ Night-soil, two years old,
- ⅓ Leaf-mould,
- ⅒ Sea, or river sand

To be well prepared and incorporated.[19]

The mind boggles, but these ingredients were readily at hand then and worked very well together when mixed into compost. Today, thankfully, a range of hygienic and altogether more suitable ingredients are used. But beyond those early dark times materials such as fibrous loam were made by stacking regular-sized sods from the top spit of turf that had been habitually grazed by livestock green-side down. Sometimes farmyard manure was added and the lot was covered with old carpeting or disused rugs. Planks of timber or whatever else was deemed suitable were then used to stabilize the pile and it was left to rot down for two or three years. When the resultant loam was ready and needed it was chopped or dug away for use and mixed with leaf mould and sand in varying proportions.

Home-mixed composts

Not so many years ago young apprentice gardeners, working on large estate gardens, would sometimes have the task of mixing various composts using field-collected loam that had been sterilized overnight in a mobile steam sterilizer. The loam was shovelled into the sterilizer at the end of the working day, the fire lit and the whole thing left to cook overnight. The sweet earthy aroma as the doors of the sterilizer were opened first thing the next morning is a smell not to be forgotten. The compost mixes were much as the same as the standard John Innes composts.

John Innes Composts

The standard mix formula contains:

- seven parts of sterilized loam
- three parts of sphagnum moss peat or leaf mould
- two parts of silver sand

Depending on the type of compost various quantities of the following are also added:

- ground limestone
- hoof and horn meal
- superphosphate
- potassium sulphate (also known as sulphate of potash)

John Innes composts are a tried and tested formula using standard ingredients to give the majority of plants a healthy constitution.

All of the compost required would have been mixed manually for all of the seed-sowing of annual bedding plants and vegetable plants under protection, the pricking out of thousands of seedlings, or for potting on and the re-potting of house plants and foliage plants for display purposes. During the course of a season, many tons would be mixed this way.

In an era of 'make do and mend' all plant pots and seed trays were reused. They would be washed in dimly lit potting sheds, or outdoors, in the quieter winter months, most often with cold water from a standpipe.

The sterilized loam was sieved and mixed with riddled leaf mould, which added the fibrous element to the composts. The leaves had been collected in autumn and winter and stacked open to the elements in a chicken-wire compound to be used when required. The leaves were predominantly oak along with leaves of some other trees such as ash and chestnut. They took quite a lot of time to rot down – at least two years and often longer.

Today the job can be speeded up by putting the collected leaves through a petrol-powered garden shredder. By using one of these machines in just a year the leaves will have rotted down sufficiently for use in composts. If a machine is not available then a handful of ammonium sulphate per square metre of leaves will really speed up the rotting process.

Occasionally a proportion of sphagnum moss peat would also be incorporated or used as a substitute for leaf mould. Washed sand, grit and John Innes base fertilizer or a cocktail of inorganic and organic fertilizers and lime were also added. The resulting compost was, without a doubt, a very good alternative to any proprietary brand, and more economical too. It would be mixed in copious quantities on large wooden boards or on the concrete floor of open-fronted potting sheds. As with mortar-making it was turned, watered carefully and turned again, ameliorating all the time.

The use of peat alone or in compost mixes is today frowned upon by the environmentally friendly. A substitute that is on a par with peat has yet to be discovered or invented, as the water and nutrient holding capacity of peat is unequalled. Various substitutes are being trialled and are used both commercially and in the amateur market.

Coconut fibre (coir) is the predominant alternative, with other materials still not making the grade. Amateur gardeners use 69 per cent of all peat used in Great Britain, with around 43 per cent of peat used here originating in the UK. Auricula growers are, naturally, a part of this demographic but peat is not generally the main constituent of auricula compost – although it is a constituent of John Innes compost mixes, of course.

Thankfully, modern composts are a far cry from what they were in Mr Kenney's era! As far as composts suitable for auriculas are concerned then it is true to say that there is no one right compost mix for

Leaf Mould

- Leaf mould can be used as a substitute for peat, so it is environmentally more friendly.
- It makes a great mulch.
- It is a good soil conditioner that enhances the organic matter content of the soil, so increasing water and nutrient retention.
- Leaves from most deciduous trees can be used, but not sycamore because it can carry the disease anthracnose.
- Do not use evergreen leaves as they will not break down.
- Do not use clippings from cypress trees, which will upset the pH balance of the soil.

Compost Mixes for Auricula Growers

An auricula potting compost:

- one part John Innes No.2 compost
- one part multi-purpose compost
- one part 3mm potting grit, or vermiculite.

An alternative auricula potting compost:

- two parts John Innes No.2 compost
- one part multi-purpose compost
- one part 3mm potting grit or vermiculite.

An auricula seed and cutting compost:

- one part sieved John Innes No.2 compost
- one part washed silver sand, or vermiculite.

A favourite compost for potting on and re-potting:

- one pail of John Innes No.2 compost
- one pail of good multi-purpose compost
- one litre-pot of 3–6mm potting grit
- one litre of silver sand
- a dessert spoon of crushed charcoal
- half a dessert spoon of the organic-based fish, blood and bone fertilizer, or a quarter dessert spoon of Q4 inorganic fertilizer.

them; indeed, there are quite a few recipes recommended by experienced growers, varying a little here and there. Probably the most important factor is that they all have an open nature, allowing good drainage, and to this end it will be noted there is always grit added. In their natural environment auriculas enjoy perfect drainage and as auricula growers we need to aim to replicate these conditions as far as possible.

Proprietary multi-purpose compost bought from your local garden centre or supermarket is definitely the wrong compost for auriculas. The peat or peat substitute in these composts hold a lot of water, which is an attribute that is ideal for most garden plants but is absolutely not for alpine plants. The retained water, especially when allied to cool weather conditions, will rot the roots of alpines and soon lead to their death. Conversely, during the warmer months very wet compost combined with warm temperatures will lead to balmy conditions in and around the pots, which will more than likely see the demise of your auriculas through the invasion of mould.

There are bags of special alpine compost available at some retail outlets, but I recommend a home-made mixture to ensure the correct ratio of ingredients to suit you. An easy test to determine if compost is near suitable for alpines is to take a handful of the material and squeeze; if the compost stays together firmly in a ball then it is not suitable as a growing medium for any alpine plant but, on the other hand, if the material readily crumbles then it is compost that is more suitable for the growing of alpines, including auriculas.

Potting grit.

Multi-purpose compost.

John Innes No 2 compost.

Silver sand.

POTS

Auriculas are generally grown in plastic pots as the more traditional clays pots, the 'Long Tom' as used by auricula growers of old, are now scarce. The plastic pot sizes most often used for auricula growing are 2½in (65mm), 3in (75mm) and 3½in (90mm). The 3in pots are the same measurement in depth, whereas the Long Tom of the Victorian age tended to be 3in in diameter and have a depth of practically 4in. A greater depth of pot is conducive to deeper rooting, making the auricula work harder and so causing a

'Argus' in a 'Long Tom' clay pot.

consequential increase in top growth.

These old clay pots are more traditional and certainly more aesthetically appealing. Arguably their chief disadvantage is their fragility as once broken they cannot be put back together satisfactorily. Broken pieces may be glued back together but they never look quite the same of course, and they are likely to break again at that spot.

Also, owing to their natural texture, these pots are more porous and so lose moisture far more quickly than plastic pots, although this apparent disadvantage can be an advantage for auricula growing as the compost inside the clay pot will not be too wet for long. However, because of this auriculas grown in them will require watering more often, which can be a problem when the grower is away from his or her collection for a few days or more and he or she has to rely on others to carry out necessary watering. Stains will eventually appear on the outsides of clay pots, which can look pleasing by adding a look of rustication, but moulds and mosses too may also grow on the outsides of the pots. These are easily removed, however, with a stiff handheld brush taken to the affected pots.

As said previously, auriculas should not be over-potted as they perform far better when there is a good and full root system in the pot. A root system that finds itself with a lot of compost to grow through before it reaches the edge

Victorian 'Long Toms'.

of the pot is more likely to suffer from water logging and resultant death by root rot, as the compost remains wet with not enough roots are present to absorb excess moisture.

To the keen auricula grower the aesthetics of the pots is important and so auriculas are generally displayed at the auricula shows in clay pots. Auriculas grown in clay pots do look more natural than those housed in plastic pots, despite the terracotta colouring of plastics. If you are fortunate enough to obtain some Long Tom clays from the Victorian era then the rim of the pots may well have chipped areas, and may have patchy colouration, but this, in my opinion, makes them look even better.

The Benefits of Using Clay Pots

- Clay pots are traditional.
- Clay pots keep auriculas drier than plastic pots.
- Clay pots are aesthetically more appealing than plastic pots and are preferred for displaying at the auricula shows.
- When they have been used for a while clay pots take on a rustic look.
- Pot-plant saucers made in clay compliment clay pots very well.
- Clay pots are available through good garden centres and horticultural suppliers via the Internet.

When you have purchased your clay pots a little preparation is required before use. It is a very good idea and common practice among enthusiasts to immerse clay pots in a bucket of water before they are first used – this is because when a dry clay pot is filled with compost the terracotta will act as a wick and displace moisture from the compost too quickly before the plant has had a chance to settle down. In order to prevent this the pots should be immersed completely in water until there are no more air bubbles rising from them. Overnight soaking is preferable, but an hour is probably the minimum necessary time.

The maximum pot size in which to grow auriculas is generally the 9F or 3½in diameter pot, but some professional growers will use

Traditional Clay Flower Pot Sizes

Clay flower pots are traditionally graded according to size and were given names accordingly. Auricula Victorian Long Toms are 3in (75mm) in diameter and 3¾ to 4in (95–100mm) in depth. The following list shows the diameter size of typical traditional pots:

Name	Diameter in inches
Thumbs or Nineties (90s)	1
Thimbles or Seventy-Twos (72s)	2½
Sixties (60s)	3
Forty-Eights (48s)	4½
Thirty-Twos (32s)	6
Sixteens (16s)	9½
Eights (8s)	12
Sixes (6s)	13
Fours (4s)	15

Plastic Flower Pot Sizes

Code	Size
6E	2in (50mm)
6F	2¼in (57mm)
8F	3in (75mm)
9F	3½in (90mm)
10F	4in (100mm)

Self auricula 'Nefertiti'.

sizes up to one litre deep plastic pots for the more vigorous varieties. This method of potting on is only advisable for use by very experienced amateur growers.

WATERING AND FERTILIZATION

First and foremost it must be said that auriculas grown in pots must on no account become waterlogged, at any time of the year, ever. If they do then death is almost guaranteed.

As mentioned in Chapter 1, the natural home of the *P. auricula* is the Alps of France (the Jura and Vosges), the mountainous regions of the Black Forest of Germany and the Tatra mountains between Poland and Slovakia. Growing at altitudes of at least 1,000m and 1,500m above sea level, it is clear that the soil conditions in which they flourish can be very different to the type of soil most of us have in our gardens. Their root zone will have perfect drainage for their needs and adequate mineral reserves for their nutritional requirements.

Alpine soils are found in the mountainous regions above the natural sub-alpine tree line. There is a lack of trees, however, in the high-altitude belt, which is a predominantly continuous grass carpet where alpine flowers flourish. A large range of soil types exists in the Alps owing to the topographical conditions, development over time and the parent material.

The common feature to differing alpine soils is that they are all influenced by the periglacial environment. As a result of the last glaciation alpine soils are relatively young, at less than 10,000 years BP (before present). On the steep slopes the soils tend to be thin, often truncated, and in a constant process of renewal. There are also deep soils in some alpine meadows and these are under threat from overgrazing, climate change and acid depositons over time.

It is in the high pastures

and rocky outcrops that the genus *Primula* thrives. It is to be reasoned that at such an elevation and with rocky and stony conditions ground water-logging will not occur. In order to grow auriculas ourselves satisfactorily then these factors should be borne in mind.

It is hard-wired into auriculas that prolonged wet soil conditions are not tolerated. In their natural home just below the glacial line they are covered, and therefore protected, by snow for a long part of the alpine winter. As auricula enthusiasts we have to replicate as far as possible these conditions of the alpine habitat in order to keep our auriculas in good shape – except by creating snow of course! If planted in the garden they should be in a well-drained soil of moderate fertility (that is, not too full of organic material) and preferably out of the bright sun but not too shaded. Ensure the soil does not waterlog, as a properly constructed alpine bed or rockery would not. If they are to be planted in pots for frame or greenhouse culture then a free-draining compost mix is necessary.

Watering

There is no one right way to water auriculas, just as there is no one correct compost mix; it is a question of personal preference. During the late spring and summer months auriculas may be watered from the top using a culinary baster. This method is more time consuming than using a long spouted watering can but

---

Indicators for When Watering is Required

- When the surface of the compost is a pale colour.
- When the leaves are flaccid (but this is not to be confused when the plants are wilting from heat).
- When the weight of the pot feels significantly lighter than when adequate moisture was present.
- When the compost has shrunk away from the pot sides.

On the latter point, when watering again the water will flow through the pots very quickly. It is better to stand these pots in trays of water to enable them to absorb from the bottom until sufficient is taken up.

---

it is less dangerous in terms of water splashing onto the foliage, especially when the can is fairly full. This is not so critical in the summer months when the higher temperatures will evaporate the water quite quickly. During the cooler months water spillage can be disastrous, however. Beware of watering unnecessarily just because you think it should be done.

During prolonged spells of very warm weather auriculas can be placed on top of capillary matting in large, shallow garden trays on greenhouse benches. The matting acts as a reservoir, with the auricula roots drawing the water they require through the process of osmosis. As the temperatures steadily rise as the year goes

on the transpiration rate follows suit, reaching its highest point usually in mid-summer. It is then that this method of watering comes into its own by saving a lot of time. The auriculas may need watering two or three times per week now.

Later in the year, when the water requirement is a lot less, place the pots in pans or bowls of water for only a matter of a seconds – this is all it takes to penetrate the compost adequately when the pots are held to just below their rims. With experience you will develop a feel for when they have had sufficient water by their weight and your memory. When watering by this method it is easy to add fungicide, insecticide or liquid fertilizer to the water as needed.

Factors Affecting Loss of Moisture from the Compost

- The plant size: a larger plant has a bigger root system and so will absorb water more quickly than a smaller specimen.
- The pot material: as clay is porous the water loss is greater than if using plastic pots. It is not easy to over-water plants in clay pots.
- The temperature: the plant and compost dries out at a faster rate in periods of warmer weather.
- The root growth: more roots result in more moisture absorption.
- The organic content of the compost.

A word or two of caution: capillary matting serves a useful purpose but care must be exercised in its use. Too much water, especially at or near the carrot, may cause rot if your auriculas are stood on sodden capillary matting for too long. If using this matting take care not to over-apply water – this should be gauged very carefully, especially if you are to leave the auriculas for any length of time. Overwatering is probably the main reason for auriculas loss. If you are away for significant periods of time then ensure you have a trusted person who understands auricula requirements and is well drilled before you leave. There is nothing worse than returning home to find your trusted person has been over-zealous.

Rainwater

By all means collect rainwater in water butts or open-top containers. Connected to a downspout from a pitched roof, water butts are generally available in sizes of 22 gallons (100 litres), 30 gallons (136 litres) and 46 gallons (210 litres). Most are barrel-shaped but some are available in a rounded-off square shape which allows for placing into corners for a snug fit. They are all manufactured from recycled plastic materials. Water butt stands will raise them off the ground and allow easy access to a fitted tap. It is important to mention that if using open-top containers ensure there is no access for children.

Water butts are handy for collecting rainwater.

Fertilizers

At around the end of February and into early March is the time when auricula growers will start to encourage healthy growth by feeding their plants with a liquid fertilizer. Use a product which is quite high in the potash element, such as a 5:2.5:10 ratio of N:P:K (nitrogen to phosphorous to potassium), for liquid fertilizing auriculas. This formulation is sold as a tomato fertilizer and is generally applied to tomatoes after the first truss of fruit has set. Do not be put off that the bottle states it to be tomato fertilizer, the product is basically a liquid fertilizer that is suitable for all flowers owing to the higher percentage of potash to assist flowering performance.

Some auricula growers use this fertilizer at a diluted strength of approximately 50 per cent of the recommended rate at each watering from the start of the March. There are other liquid fertilizers on the market at a higher strength than the 5:2.5:10, and if these are used then further dilution would be required. Undiluted they are too strong for auriculas but fine if you are growing tomatoes or sunflowers. It would be more appropriate to use one of these products at a quarter-strength solution. For the double auriculas, however, it is suggested a liquid fertilizer such as the 5:2.5:10 be used at a normal dilution rate, as this type of auricula tends to need more nourishment than the other types.

BASE FERTILIZERS FOR COMPOST MIXING

As far as base fertilizers for compost mixes are concerned then either fish, blood and bone, which is organically derived, or Q4, which has added trace elements but is inorganic, could be added at the rate of half a dessertspoon to a compost mix. Some growers rely on the fertilizer that is all ready present in John Innes fertilizers so they add no extra.

The nutrient composition and ratio of fish, blood and bone is: 5 per cent nitrogen (N), 5 per cent phosphorous (P) and 6.5 per cent potassium (K). As this balanced fertilizer is organically derived then, of course, it is available to plants in a controlled-release form. The nitrogen and phosphoric elements in this blended fertilizer are obtained from

Mineral Nutrients for Growth

Macronutrients:

- **N**: Nitrogen is the mineral element that provides stem and leaf growth. It is easily leached from the soil after rainfall and needs to be replenished regularly in the growing season. A deficiency is recognized by pale foliage and checked growth.
- **P**: Phosphorous is the mineral element that is required for a healthy and vigorous root system. A deficiency is seen by spindly growth and small lower leaves of a dark green colouration with yellowing edges.
- **K**: Potash or potassium is the mineral element that helps provide overall plant hardiness and flowering potential. A deficiency is noted by reduced flower size in severe cases, and a yellowing of the foliage.
- **C**: Calcium is required for healthy cell membranes, particularly within the root system. A deficiency is manifested by short plant growth and yellowing foliage.
- **Mg**: Magnesium is needed as an enzyme activator and is a major part of the chlorophyll molecule. A deficiency causes pale foliage and flowers.
- **S**: Sulphur is part of two amino acids that are components of plant proteins. A deficiency is much the same as for a lack of nitrogen.

Micronutrients:

Boron (B), chlorine (Cl), iron (Fe), manganese (Mn), zinc (Zn) and molybdenum (Mo).
These elements are all required by plants for healthy growth but only in trace amounts.

Border auricula 'Dales Red'.

animal material, whereas the potash element is from the inorganic muriate of potash or sulphate of potash (potassium sulphate).

So it is evident that fish, blood and bone is really an organic-based and not a truly organic fertilizer, but for all that it is the best choice for the auricula grower. Owing to its organic nature it breaks down more slowly than an inorganic fertilizer and therefore is effective over a longer period of time. It promotes strong growth, healthy foliage and a good root system.

The Q4 inorganic fertilizer has an NPK analysis of: 5.3:7.5:10 with added trace elements. It is a quite a bit stronger and faster acting than fish, blood and bone, and is considered, by some, as too strong in the potash element for auriculas and other members of the *Primula* genus.

GROWING AURICULAS IN THE GARDEN

Auriculas are mainly grown by enthusiasts in glasshouses or cold frames, but two types of auricula will give a lovely display when grown in beds or borders in the garden.

Both the alpine and border types will withstand severe winter weather and sustain little damage. The flowers and leaves will not suffer in their quality as would the show types, with the farina on the foliage being ruined easily by rainfall. Auriculas in the garden will be very much at home when planted with other alpine and rockery plants.

It is not often that a gardener will be fortunate enough to have a raised area in the garden that can made to look like a natural rocky outcrop, so a purpose-made rock garden will have to be constructed.

How to Make an Alpine Trough

- Paint the surface of an old glazed sink unit with a black bitumen sealer or fibreglass kit.
- Mix two parts of sharp sand, one part of Portland cement and one part of fine grade damp peat.
- Apply all over the sink to a depth of around 1in (25mm) and lightly ripple the surface.
- Once dried paint on natural yoghurt, this will soon encourage the formation of mosses and lichens to give the desired rustic look.

This can be done on a suitable flat area in your garden by excavating a pathway and using the removed soil to fill under, between and behind rocks.

A raised bed constructed of rock and soil is ideal for cascading subjects such as *Lithodora* 'Heavenly Blue' or *Saponaria officinalis*.

Plant auriculas towards the top of rockeries where there will be more drainage owing to the height. Pockets should be formed between the individual rocks, allowing flexibility for using differing soil types if required. Try to source rock material that has been quarried nearest to your home. To use, say, Westmorland rock in an area where sandstone is prevalent would be inappropriate. Of course, cost considerations do come into the equation and rocks are not inexpensive.

An alternative to rock is a substance called Tufa. This is formed in some limestone regions and is composed of calcium carbonate. It is porous and lightweight and provides a good anchorage for some plants. Whichever rocks are used, they need to be laid with their longest dimension in a horizontal position. This is how the material is fractured naturally by the weather and it deserves to be placed sympathetically. Do not place the rocks vertically; you are not trying to recreate Stonehenge!

Apart from rock gardens, alpine subjects are easier to maintain when grown in containers. Ideally stone troughs should be used, but the price of them is prohibitive for most gardeners. An alternative is to convert a disused kitchen sink to look like a stone trough.

Soil

The soil type is an important factor when constructing a rockery. It may be that your soil is ideally suited to growing alpine plants, by being of an open free-draining nature as determined by the soil texture, that is the soil's proportions of sand, silt and clay. An ideal soil for growing most garden plants is defined as a loam soil, which consists of approximately 40 per cent sand, 40 per cent silt and 20 per cent clay particles. A soil consisting of a quantity of sand particles of around 60 per cent, silt of 30 per cent and clay of 20 per cent content would be ideal for auriculas, enabling very good drainage. A soil analysis would reveal a small proportion of organic

Classification of Soils

Type	Diameter of particles
Sandy	2.0–0.2mm
Fine sand	0.2–0.02mm
Silt	0.02–0.002mm
Clay	0.002mm and lower

The Major Types of Soil

Clay soils: These have poor workability as they are sticky when wet. They are composed of very fine particles with few air spaces. These soils shrink and crack when dry and warm up slowly.

Sandy soils: These are formed of quartz, shale, silica and granite. They have large air spaces between particles. They drain freely so are susceptible during droughts. They have good workability when improved with organic material.

Silty soils: These are composed of the same particles as sands but have small air spaces, allowing them to hold water and nutrients well. They tend to block drains.

Chalky soils: Chalky soils are alkaline in nature so acid-loving plants will not thrive. Some nutrients are locked up, leaving them unavailable to plants. This type of soil requires the regular addition of organic matter and fertilizers.

Peaty soils: These tend to be more acidic and inert, but when improved with fertilizers they make a good workable soil. These soils retain water well.

Add grit to heavy soil to improve the quality.

matter, which is important for the soil structure and water and nutrient holding capabilities. A soil pH level of between 5.5 and 6.5 is ideal for auriculas and other alpine subjects.

It may be that you will have to import a better quality soil if your garden soil is of a heavy nature. Clay soils may be improved by adding organic matter in the form of well-rotted farmyard manure, home-produced compost, poultry manure or peat. To further ameliorate the heavy soil, add potting gravel and silver sand.

Companion planting

Auriculas do not have to be grown alone in a rockery or garden containers. They are very much at home when planted with other rockery or low-growing subjects in beds or borders. Consider planting them alongside *Sempervivums*, which will provide a contrast between the sometimes spiky and varying-coloured foliage of the *Sempervivums* and the mid-green leaves of the auriculas.

During the autumn auriculas will start to die down and look nothing like the vibrant plants of the spring and summer. Leaves start to yellow and the whole plant begins to look very tired. A little light application of top dressing (auricula seed compost is ideal for this) will tidy up the appearance and allow roots from the exposed carrots to take hold in the new compost.

Unnamed white border auricula in spring.

Companion Plants for Auriculas

- *Alyssum saxatile* 'Citrinum'
- *Armeria maritima* (sea thrift)
- *Artemisia stellarana* 'Mori's Form'
- *Corydalis flexuosa* 'Purple Leaf'
- *Cyclamen coum*
- *Dianthus deltoides* (maiden pink)
- *Erodium reichardii* (cranesbill)
- *Ipheion uniflorum* 'Alberto Castillo'
- *Isotoma* 'Fairy Carpet'
- *Leontopodium alpinum* (eidelweiss)
- *Lithodora* 'Blue Star' or 'Heavenly Blue'
- *Muscari hyacinthoides*
- *Scilla bifolia*
- *Scilla siberica*
- *Sempervivum* (to complement the foliage of these succulents)
- *Soldanella alpina* and *S. Villosa*
- *Synthyris stellata*
- *Viola* 'Blue Seal'
- *Viola* 'Ripple' series.

Unnamed white border auricula in October.

4 Propagation and Breeding of New Auricula Cultivars

The equipment needed in order to increase a collection of auriculas by propagation is really quite simple:

- 2in or 2¼in (50 and 57mm) and 3in (75mm) plastic flower pots
- white plastic pot plant labels
- a pencil and black permanent fine marker pen
- a notebook
- a magnifying glass
- a scalpel
- a camel hair paintbrush
- hormone rooting powder or gel
- yellow sulphur dust.

These are the basic requirements. Ensure you keep a notebook to record your propagation details. These will be the names of cultivars used for crossing, the date and perhaps further details such as the compost mixture.

If you are a new auricula grower you may be unsure whether you have the necessary skill to take offsets and grow them on successfully, but there is no difficulty at all. Have a clear idea as to what you want to achieve, keep accurate records and have patience. These are the three main attributes that should ensure success. Propagating from your own stock is the most cost effective way of producing new auriculas and is a very pleasurable challenge.

OPPOSITE PAGE:
Alpine auricula 'Sir John'.

Auricula propagation kit.

TIMING

The optimum time for auricula propagation is just after flowering in early summer and the process can carry on up until early autumn. Most offsets are produced during this period of the year.

Auriculas do not come true from seed and therefore the only way to increase your stock of named varieties is to take offsets from these cultivars. Offsets are miniature plants, or plantlets, that grow low down on the stem of auriculas. Quite often they are covered by the leaves of mature plants and because of this may be a little drawn, but these can still be used successfully for propagation.

Different auricula cultivars produce differing amounts of offsets, with some show varieties giving off only one or two offsets per year, if that, whereas others will provide an abundance of offsets throughout the growing season. The scarcity of some show cultivars on the market is because of the slowness of some plants to produce any quantity of young offsets. Some companies are producing auriculas by means of micro-propagation but there are difficulties and objections from traditionalists as to the veracity of this method of increasing auricula stock. So it will be seen that increasing one's stock can be a slow process, but thoroughly worthwhile if patience is exercised.

TAKING OFFSETS

Offsets are attached quite low down on the main stem and with care it is possible to tease them away from the parent plant with most if not all of the roots attached. If there are no roots, which is the case with offsets produced a little further up the stem, cut them away from the mother plant with a scalpel or very sharp knife and, in order to heal the wound, dust with flowers of sulphur. Offsets may be pulled away from the parent plant with careful fingers. Carefully remove the small low down leaf material towards the base of the offsets, and dip them to a depth of about 8mm in fresh hormone rooting powder or gel – using a hormone agent will encourage the early formation of roots.

Half fill the pots with compost and place the offsets, rooted or unrooted, around the edge of the 2in or 2¼in (50–57mm) flower pots, or use 3in (75mm) ones for larger sized offsets. Add more compost up to the first true leaves. Gently firm the compost, which should moist but not too wet.

Insert well-marked plant labels and finally place the pots in a shady area of your greenhouse or cold frame. Keep an eye on the pots and offsets and water carefully from beneath if wilting occurs. However, the unrooted offsets should not require further watering until rooting has taken place.

Bell jars or clear plastic pot plant covers, or a propagation

Splitting auricula offsets.

Auricula offsets divided.

case lid, may be placed over the pots in order to create a humid atmosphere to minimize moisture loss. Take great care, if using this method, to keep the surface of the cover free from a build-up of water droplets that could fall onto the offsets causing them to rot.

Rooting will generally take place in a period of approximately three weeks, if not a little sooner. New growth is the tell-tale sign that rooting has occurred, but do not be tempted to upend the pot to check for rooting at this stage. Exercise patience by waiting until the new plants are actively growing. Generally, auriculas root readily with only very occasional losses.

Allow a further minimum of two weeks after rooting has taken place before you pot up the rooted offsets into individual plant pots. Pre-rooted auricula offsets may be potted into small pots without the need for a hormone agent. These pre-rooted offsets will obviously grow more quickly than unrooted offsets.

Offsets on edge of pots.

Important Tip

By inserting offsets around the edges of the pots you will be ensuring that the roots come into contact with the pot walls at the earliest opportunity. This is very important, as when there is a long distance between roots and pot edges there is more likelihood of the offsets rotting off if the compost is too wet. Always ensure the compost is of a free-draining nature.

Offset potted.

Two well rooted offsets.

Peat plugs

The use of compressed peat plugs (the major manufacturers are trialling a coir-based alternative) is a different tried-and-tested method to using pots and composts to increase your auricula collection.
Peat plugs are purchased as flattened discs that will need to be soaked in water in order for them to expand. The advantage of using peat plugs is that the whole operation is speeded up as there is no compost to be mixed and pots to be filled. This method may be advantageous when taking offsets on a large scale. The peat discs are clean and sterile and as such cut down the risk of infection by soil-borne diseases.

Place the peat discs in seed trays and water them moderately well with a watering can. After rehydration, which occurs after approximately twenty minutes, carefully squeeze out excess water from the plugs by pressing their tops with an empty plant pot or seed tray. Retain the mesh around the outside of the peat plugs as this will give stability to the expanded peat. Next the ready-to-use expanded plugs will need to have channels scooped out by using a dibber or pencil end ready for the insertion of the auricula offsets.

Insert well-marked plant labels and insert one offset per peat plug towards the edge of the disc. Use a pencil end or dibber carefully to bring the peat material to the offset stem and firm carefully. Check morning and evenings and, as with the compost and pot method, place them in a shaded area of your greenhouse or garden frame. Under the greenhouse bench is a good place, but take care when watering the plants above that water does not drip onto the pots.

Topping

Another method of propagation, which is not often practised, is the method known as topping. This involves cutting off the top from a mature auricula plant, just above the level of compost in the pot, removing the lower leaves and using the resultant material as an unrooted cutting. This method will also provide new offsets that will be formed from the base of the remaining plant material left in the plant pot after the top removal. Often a larger number of offsets are produced this way and it can be a good way of increasing one's stock.

Before propagation operations begin, ensure that all of the necessary equipment is clean and sterilized. Labels, plant pots, seed trays, a scalpel or sharp knife and dibbers can

The Different Ways to Propagate Auriculas

- By taking pre-rooted healthy-looking offsets from the donor plant.
- By taking unrooted offsets (cuttings) and using hormone rooting powder or gel to encourage root formation.
- By seed, sowing from your own collected auricula seed or purchased seed.
- By using the topping technique.
- By using a hobbyist's tissue culture kit.
- By carefully splitting up large clumps of the border or alpine types from the garden.

all be washed and then soaked in a household sterilent. Also make certain that 3in white plastic labels are marked clearly with the parent plant name together with the date, in pencil or a fine-grade permanent ink pen. There is nothing as frustrating as finding yourself with unlabelled plants; no matter how good your memory is you *will* forget names. The idea is to be deliberate, methodical and thorough in your propagation endeavours: in short, be professional. Having this mentality is a prerequisite if you are thinking of entering your plants at the auricula flower shows. Attention to detail cannot be stressed enough.

COMMERCIAL PROPAGATION

As mentioned before, some large nurseries or institutions practise a propagation technique known as micro-propagation, otherwise known as tissue culture. This scientific method of propagation produces numerous new plants from very small plant components, and begins with the use of clean, virus-free and fungus-free plant material. This cleanliness is vitally important in the production of healthy new plants in order to prevent passing on nascent disease to new plants. The type of tissue used may be stem tips, the anthers, petals, or even plant pollen.

The plant material is cleaned and sterilized by using bleaches and alcohol washes and is finally sluiced in sterilized water. The small portions of plant tissue are then placed onto a growing medium that includes sucrose and plant hormones and this is then placed *in vitro*, that is, a sterile atmosphere. When the material has produced new plants, which will be uniform in growth, they are grown on in a traditional compost mixture and gradually hardened off to a normal growing environment.

Micro-propagation has its place in commercial horticulture for increasing virus-free plants in large numbers; as far as auriculas are concerned it is known that only relatively small quantities of named varieties have been propagated by this method. This process has been useful for reinvigorating some older and more scarce varieties.

An indication as to whether an auricula has been produced by micro-propagation is by the numerous offsets it later produces. An auricula from this background throws up so many offsets that the parent plants often become overcrowded in their pots. Hobbyist's tissue culture kits are available on the Internet. This is the scientific method of propagation but for many purists it is a no-go!

SEED-SOWING

Start to collect seed from your auricula plants from mid-summer onwards. The optimum time for seed harvest will be ascertained by the colour of the seed pods; the pods will have changed from a light green colour to brown and it is after this stage that the pod will begin to get ready to split and distribute the seed naturally. Intervene now, if you do not want the seed to fall naturally, by squeezing the seed pods gently and collecting the seed onto squares of kitchen-grade aluminium foil or paper. Clear away any detritus and store the seed in enveloped foil squares. Place these in a plastic container and leave in the bottom of the refrigerator until ready for sowing.

Generally auricula seed is sown during February or the latter part of January, however some auricula growers advocate sowing almost immediately after the seed has been harvested, when it is at its freshest. Whichever method is used no artificial heat is needed for germination. These hardy plants are not like many flowering plants from warmer climates whose seed require

Auricula seedlings under a sheet of glass.

Sources of Auricula Seed

- Your own harvested auricula seed from selected plants, either from open-pollinated plants or harvested from your crossed plant parents.
- Seed purchased via the Internet from auricula growers.
- Seed purchased from some of the commercial seed catalogue companies, although this will probably be mixed seed of different auricula types.
- Seed obtained for a small fee from the auricula societies' seed lists.
- Seed swap schemes.

a combination of moisture and bottom heat for germination.

Sow auricula seed onto seed trays or in small pots containing fresh seed compost. Sow thinly and then use a sprinkling of vermiculite or dry silver sand to just lightly cover the seeds. A light top dressing such as this assists in anchoring the radical roots as they emerge from the seed case. A carrier of sand may be mixed with the seed to facilitate sowing, but really the seeds of auriculas are large enough not to warrant this, it is a matter of choice.

Once sown the seed trays are covered with sheets of glass or clear rigid plastic, which is removed once germination has taken place. To prevent a build-up of condensation which may cause damping-off disease (see below), the glass or plastic should be removed regularly and any condensation wiped away. The seed trays or pots are placed under the greenhouse benches and left until after germination, which takes three to four weeks. Do not allow the compost to dry out, although this should not occur if it was moistened before use.

In order to prevent the occurrence of damping-off disease (*Rhizoctonia solani)* or *Pythium*, which is a root-rotting fungus, a preventative application of Bayer's Fruit and Vegetable Disease Control® may be given by watering onto the sown seed trays before they are placed under the greenhouse benches. This fungicide contains copper oxychloride and will cure damping-off disease. Use this product, which is available at garden centres and DIY outlets, at the manufacturer's recommended rate only and apply through a watering can fitted with a fine rose or a mist sprayer.

After the seedlings appear and they are large enough to handle (that is, when they have two or more leaves), they should be pricked out carefully into small pots or trays of fresh potting compost. Take the utmost care when searching for the roots of the seedlings by using a dibber or a very small culinary fork. Carefully dig deeply under the seedlings and very gently lift the plant and root mass. Transplant the seedlings to the trays or pots, where they should remain until they are large enough to be put into individual pots.

After this time pot on as the plants outgrow their containers and treat them the same as you would new auriculas raised from offsets. It will be approximately fifteen to eighteen months before flowering occurs.

BREEDING NEW CULTIVARS

There will undoubtedly come a time when in the novice grower's mind he or she becomes curious as to whether they could be lucky enough to manage to breed a show-winning new cultivar themselves. The fun of then naming their new plant and receiving the plaudits for a good job done would be very satisfying. Whether the new grower has the confidence to venture to this higher plane of auricula culture or feels that these practices are best left to the experienced hybridizers is a matter best resolved by the application of self-determination.

Some new enthusiasts aspire to create new cultivars and in time do go on to do so, and eventually exhibit these on the show benches. This should always be encouraged and, along with the dedication of the more experienced breeder, a continuity of new cultivars being introduced into the future is assured. It is thanks to the dedicated hybridizers amongst the experienced growers that new and improved varieties appear on the scene as often as they do.

Regrettably, some new cultivars eventually become poorer in form over the years and deteriorate to an extent that renders them unacceptable for showing.

Alpine auricula 'Mark'.

However, other new ones become good cultivars and continue to thrive. Some of the best-known auriculas are as good as they were when they were first introduced, whereas some others last only a matter of a few years before they drop from popularity due to diminishing quality. The breeding of new cultivars has been going on for as long as auriculas have been cultivated on these shores, and long may it continue.

It is quite probable that the new grower will want to sow seed that has been produced by his or her own insect-pollinated or hand-pollinated auriculas. Bees and other pollinating insects will have flown from pip to pip, spreading pollen as they went on their industrious and merry way. From this resultant collected seed will come a great many seedlings varying in their form and flower, but there is a chance that a really good seedling will be produced and will grow into a first-rate performer. Sometimes a good seedling will also go on to become a good parent for further hybridizing. Leaving nature to do the job of pollination is fine but the novice grower will, in all probability, want to be selective and try and breed a new variety that has certain desired characteristics.

Traits such as good overall form, a deeper or brighter colour hue, an acceptable tube of neatness and so on are some of the qualities that are desirable for passing on to a future seedling and eventual mature auricula. The cliché that Rome wasn't built in a day holds true in auricula breeding,

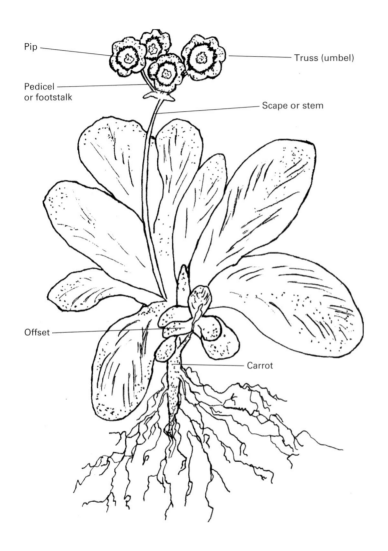

Pip

Pedicel
or footstalk

Truss (umbel)

Scape or stem

Offset

Carrot

Parts of the auricula.

as it may well take years before the grower achieves what he or she wants in a new auricula cultivar.

Records taken meticulously and kept safely are of paramount importance and this is the only way to proceed. Many old varieties have arrived with us today without any clue as to the parent plants. Records of these may have been taken and lost, or may not have been taken at all.

Hand pollination

The first thing needed is a clear idea of what one is hoping to achieve. As mentioned, good record-keeping is essential, but of equal importance is the need for the correct equipment, which is minimal, and to ensure that your pollination experiments are taken from healthy and virus-free stock. The last point must be considered as one should not

unwittingly transfer undesirable diseases to new plants.

The appropriate time for pollination is when the flowers are just half open, as this is the point at which the recipient stigma is at its most receptive. All that is needed for hand pollination is a pair of very sharp household scissors and a pair of fine-pointed tweezers or a camel-hair brush. These brushes are generally made from squirrel, pony, or goat hair, or a combination of all of these, but as long as the hair is of a fine fibre it will suffice. Using the sharp scissors cut across the flower petals of one auricula flower to include removing the stamens, this will expose the stigma ready for the pollen donation. Using either the camel-hair brush or fine-pointed tweezers, and wearing reading glasses if your eyesight needs enhancing, collect pollen from the stamens of the donor auricula (the pollen parent) – the pollen resembles farina and is of a fluffy nature when ripe – and carefully place it onto the stigma of the seed parent auricula. The stigma, at the half-open flower stage, will have exuded a sticky substance that allows the pollen to adhere to it. Care should be exercised throughout the whole operation so as not to damage the stigma.

To reiterate, hand pollination should be carried out before the flowers are fully opened in order for the operation to be successful. If the flowers have been fully open for a while when pollination is tried, then

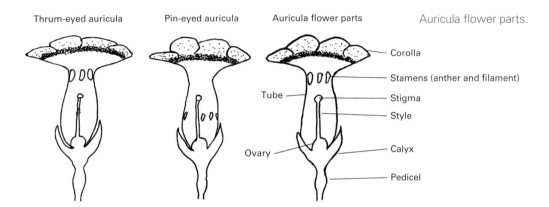

Thrum-eyed auricula

Pin-eyed auricula

Auricula flower parts

Corolla

Stamens (anther and filament)

Tube

Stigma

Style

Ovary

Calyx

Pedicel

Auricula flower parts.

attempts at this procedure at this time are likely to be doomed to failure. It cannot be stressed enough that the correct timing is essential in this procedure.

If using a camel-hair brush, ensure that after each transfer the brush is thoroughly cleansed of pollen and then sterilized. This will prevent pollen from different auriculas becoming inappropriately mixed and therefore causing cross-contamination. After this procedure, mark up a plastic label with the name of the pollen parent and seed parent and also the date of hand pollination by using a pencil or permanent fine-tipped marker pen. Attach the label to the pedicel (footstalk) of the seed parent. Also record your efforts in a purpose-used notebook or on a database on your personal computer. It is also wise and good practice to pollinate several pips on the same auricula to assist in generating plenty of seed.

Place the seed parents in a separate area of the greenhouse. The other flowers on the same plant may be removed or left to pollinate

Alpine auricula

Border auricula

Double auricula

Edged auricula

Fancy auricula

Self auricula

Striped autricula

Auricula flower types.

freely. It is a good idea and common practice to transpose the procedure by using pollen from the seed parent's stamen to pollinate the stigma of the pollen parent. This is known as back-crossing.

Another method of hand pollination is to carefully invert the pollen parent flower that has had the petals removed enough to fully expose the stamens. The stamens are then lightly wiped over the stigma of the seed parent, ensuring a good covering. Directly after hand pollination, using a magnifying glass or reading glasses, look at the stigma of the seed parent, to see if there is pollen attached to it. This will ascertain whether the transfer of pollen has been successful or not.

It will take several weeks for the seed to ripen, maybe as many as twelve, by which time the footstalk and ovary will have turned a brown colour. The seed pod, when it has started to split open a little, may be placed in a receptacle to catch the falling seed, or gently squeezed and shaken to collect the seed onto a piece of aluminium foil or paper. If not required for immediate use, then sprinkle the seed into aluminium foil squares, fold and store in a plastic box in the bottom of a refrigerator. Make certain that the seed packaging is clearly marked before storage.

Hand pollination is an exciting project to undertake but do not expect good results every time as there are many thousands of seedlings germinated each year that do not make the grade. Expectations should be realistic and when one has produced an acceptable cultivar and it goes on to win a prize on the show bench then all of the efforts will have been very worthwhile.

Alpine auricula 'Joy'.

A GALLERY OF AURICULAS

(All photographs: Drointon Nurseries of Plaster Pitts, Norton Conyers, Ripon, North Yorkshire.)

Alpine auricula 'Ice Maiden'.

Alpine auricula 'June'.

Alpine auricula 'Kingfisher'.

Alpine auricula 'Landy'.

Alpine auricula 'Mollie Langford'.

Alpine auricula 'Nikity'.

Alpine auricula 'Rowena'.

Alpine auricula 'Tally Ho'.

Alpine auricula 'Ted Gibbs'.

Border auricula 'Aubergine'.

Border auricula 'Bran'.

Border auricula 'Bush Baby'.

Border auricula 'Feuerkönig'.

Border auricula 'Harlequin'.

Border auricula 'Mrs Lowry'.

Border auricula 'My Friend'.

Border auricula 'Nancy Dalgety'.

Border auricula 'Old Yellow Dusty Miller'.

Border auricula 'Robbo'.

Border auricula 'Starling'.

Border auricula 'Winifred'.

Border auricula 'Wycliffe Harmony'.

Double auricula 'Crimson Glow'.

Double auricula 'Golden Hind'.

Double auricula 'Pegasus'.

Double auricula 'Pink Fondant'.

Double auricula 'Riatty'.

Double auricula 'Rose Conjou'.

Double auricula 'Susannah'.

Double auricula 'Trouble'.

Green edged auricula 'Chloe'.

Green edged auricula 'Colonel Champney'.

Green edged auricula 'Figaro'.

Green edged auricula 'Gleneagles'.

Green edged auricula 'Jupiter'.

Green edged auricula 'Oban'.

Green edged auricula 'Orb'.

Green edged auricula 'Prague'.

Green edged auricula 'Tamino'.

Grey edged auricula 'Almondbury'.

Grey edged auricula 'Cornmeal'.

Grey edged auricula 'Hetty Wolf'.

Grey edged auricula 'Kingpin'.

Grey edged auricula 'Minstrel'.

Grey edged auricula 'Sherwood'.

Grey edged auricula 'Teem'.

White edged auricula 'White Ensign'.

Fancy auricula 'Blue Chip'.

Fancy auricula 'Coffee'.

Fancy auricula 'Crimple'.

Fancy auricula 'Fanfare'.

Fancy auricula 'Helen Barter'.

Fancy auricula 'Hinton Fields'.

Fancy auricula 'Minley'.

Fancy auricula 'Rajah'.

Fancy auricula 'Second Vic'.

Fancy auricula 'Showtime'.

Fancy auricula 'Trafalgar Square'.

Self auricula 'Angel Islington'.

Self auricula 'Chaffinch'.

Self auricula 'Chiffon'.

Self auricula 'Lady Diana'.

Self auricula 'Joel'.

Self auricula 'Lilac Domino'.

Self auricula 'Mojave'.

Self auricula 'Old Gold'.

Self auricula 'Red Gauntlet'.

Self auricula 'Rosie'.

Self auricula 'Sailor Boy'.

Self auricula 'Scorcher'.

Self auricula 'Sunflower'.

Self auricula 'The Snods'.

Striped auricula 'Angela Short'.

Striped auricula 'Blush Baby'.

Striped auricula 'Bold Tartan'.

Striped auricula 'Marion Tiger'.

Striped auricula 'Mazetta'.

Striped auricula 'Night and Day'.

Striped auricula 'Red Wire'.

Striped auricula 'Robin Hood'.

Striped auricula 'Star Spangle'.

Striped auricula 'Violet Surprise'.

5 Pests and Diseases of Auriculas

PESTS

Generally speaking auriculas are not troubled by too many pests or diseases. However, two pests, the red spider mite and the vine weevil, can be particularly troublesome. As with all plant cultivation, vigilance must be observed at all times. Get into the habit of checking over your plants every day, not forgetting to study the undersides of the leaves. It is often here that pests will lurk, hoping not to be spotted.

The auricula is a hardy plant and if treated as such – with no exposure to artificial heat that will promote soft growth so as to make them susceptible to attack – then so much the better. Pests and diseases may well strike as soon as your back is turned, so the grower should ensure that preventative treatments are given at regular intervals, and particularly before he or she is away from their plants for a period of time.

Red spider mite *(Tetranychus urticae)*

The red spider mite, being a microscopic insect, is notoriously difficult to detect. A magnifying glass or strong reading spectacles will be needed in order to identify the pests, especially in the early days of an attack. An advanced attack will be noticeable by

OPPOSITE PAGE:
Self auricula 'Remus'.

Red spider damage to auricula foliage.

mottling and fine webbing attached to the plant's leaves.

These tell-tale signs are especially conspicuous on the older foliage of heavily mealed show auriculas such as 'Bilton', 'Helen', 'Alice Haysom' and 'April Moon' and so on. The leaves gradually turn yellow in colour and in a severe attack they will wilt.

Red spider mites feed on the sap of auriculas and other plants, and inevitably this will weaken the affected plants' constitution. Unless treated by a spraying regime, plant death is all but inevitable. The red spider mite revels in the dry and warm conditions of greenhouses or frames during the summer months.

Non-chemical treatment
In order to help prevent an outbreak, regularly dampen down the greenhouse footpath with water from a watering can fitted with a rose. This action will promote a more humid atmosphere, which will assist in deterring the red spider mite. Transferring auriculas to cold frames facing north and therefore out of the sunnier conditions will also assist with eradication.

Another non-chemical treatment is biological control by the use of predatory mites known by the name of *Phytoseiulus persimilis*. These mites are effective by feeding on the eggs and the growing stages of the red spider. The rapacious predatory mites breed extraordinarily quickly given optimum conditions, and can be expected to devour a huge quantity of red spider mites.

To be most efficient the right conditions will need to be given in the greenhouse. A regular temperature of above 21°C will need to be achieved in order for the predatory mite to out-breed the red spider mite. After October the use of this predator is far less effective as red spider invasion would naturally be diminished by this time of the year. Do not attempt to control the red spider mite with insecticides at the same time as using a predatory mite as you will kill the beneficial mites.

Chemical treatment
Regular spraying with a systemic (translocated) garden insecticide is an effective treatment. Before use always ensure you follow the directions on the product label. These types of insecticide are available from garden centres and even some supermarkets. Products containing the chemical bifenthrin will destroy red spider mite and also aphids, whitefly and caterpillars.

A note of caution: spraying auriculas can ruin the delicate farina of show and border types. It would be a wise move to carefully water the insecticide onto the surface of the compost or to apply it by adding to water and watering from the bottom of the pot.

Heavily mealed foliage of show type.

Vine weevil *(Otiorhynchus sulcatus)*

Another pest that may also attack auriculas is the very dangerous vine weevil. An invasion by this dreaded insect can be a nightmare for the auricula grower. The vine weevil in its grub stage looks very similar to the common maggot but is the shape of the letter 'C'. It has an orange head and is approximately ½in (12mm) in length. The grubs cause damage to auriculas by chewing up the roots, leading to the plant collapsing and eventually dying.

An attack will usually occur from around October to May but may also happen again in late summer or early autumn. In its adult stage the vine weevil looks like a small dark grey beetle with yellow spots on its carapace. This particular nasty will happily nibble away on the leaves, leaving them lacerated and shredded. The plants will also look very wilted, much as if they had been left to get too dry.

Search these pests out, and collect and destroy them immediately on the spot. The vine weevil hides away during daylight hours and only emerges at night to munch away on unsuspecting plants, so vigilance must be observed. Night visits to your greenhouse or frames are recommended with a torch to check during the evenings or night if an attack is suspected.

This pest in its adult form may be detected scurrying around on the top of and under the pots. If found, gather them up and dispose of immediately – a quick dispatch is highly recommended! The night-feeding vine weevil lays its eggs on the surface of the plant compost. The emerged larvae tunnels its way into the compost in search of food, which will be the roots of your prized auriculas. They will happily and indiscriminately eat away at the roots, carrots and any emerged offsets.

Non-chemical treatment
Always purchase auriculas, and any other plant for that matter, from a reputable source. It is advisable to check the rootball at the earliest opportunity for signs of vine weevil. If there are grubs in the root system

then shake them off, destroy and then re-pot the auriculas in fresh compost. Get rid of the infected compost: *do not place it in your compost bin but dispose of it away from your garden as soon as possible*.

The use of biological control and eradication is another method for the grower, and is based on the use of nematodes. These tiny worms, *Steinernema kraussei*, are microscopic creatures that enter the bodies of the vine weevil grubs. Once there, they emit bacteria that will poison and kill them. The nematodes multiply over the summer months and the young later join in on the attack on vine weevil grubs.

An application of nematodes should be made in March to protect the plants for the summer months, and a further application made in the autumn. They are available from several mail order suppliers who advertise in the gardening press.

Chemical treatment
This pernicious bug can be treated with chemical formulations containing the chemicals chlorpyrifos, thiacloprid or acetamiprid. Some compost manufacturers add an insecticide to their compost mixes that goes by the name of Suscon Green. This is a controlled-release granular soil insecticide that contains 10 per cent chlorpyrifos. The compost costs a little more than brands without chlorpyrifos, but the benefits outweigh the few extra pennies spent. The

chemical is effective for up to two years in containerized plants.

Provado® Vine Weevil Killer 2 contains 9g/lt of systemic insecticide thiacloprid. This chemical can be used for any container-grown plants (apart from edible ones), and comes in liquid form that needs to be diluted with water. It may be applied as a drench to the surface of the compost in the pot, or given to the plants from under the pots by standing them briefly in trays. In order to provide complete protection, first apply a solution in spring when your auriculas are growing rapidly followed by a further application four months later and a final application four months after that. This regime will give year-round protection.

Provado will also give some protection against whitefly, greenfly and blackfly. A proprietary chemical spray that contains acetamiprid will have a similar effect as Provado, and will also control aphids.

Whitefly *(Trialeurodes vaporariorum)*

Whitefly is a very small and destructive pest that invades the upper and lower sides of foliage and feeds on the new shoots of plants by sucking away at the sap. By this process of sap-sucking the plant becomes weakened and will lose its defences against infections and also attack by other insects. The female adult whitefly lays eggs which hatch into minute white scales that adhere to the undersides of the leaves.

Not content with sucking the life out of your auriculas, whitefly will also display appalling toilet manners and excrete all over the foliage. The resulting sticky substance plays host to sooty mould (*see* 'Diseases'), which disfigures the plant and eventually inhibits the process of photosynthesis.

Non-chemical treatment
Suspend insect glue-traps over the top of the plants in the greenhouse. These oblong yellow plastic cards are coated in a non-harmful glue. The yellow colouring of the traps attracts flying insects; not only will whitefly get caught on them but a myriad other flying insects will too. After spring and summer the oblong plastic traps will be covered with the remains of all manner of flying insects, leaving little room for any more unsuspecting pests. Remove and destroy all used traps and replace them the following spring.

Another alternative to the chemical route for control or eradication is the use of biological methods. The predatory and parasitic wasp *Encarsia formosa* lays its eggs in the whitefly scales, from where they hatch and then kill their host. This parasitic wasp searches out more scales and keeps destroying them until the supply of whitefly is stopped. The life cycle then halts and more *Encarsia* will have to be introduced if further outbreaks of whitefly invasion occur.

This method of treatment has been around for many years in commercial horticultural operations and is becoming more common in use among gardeners. The *Encarsia* are supplied as pupae on cards that should be suspended over the auriculas. For their most effective use, temperatures need to be at least 18°C during the day and 14°C at night. Do not use insecticides whilst *Encarsia* is operating in your greenhouse, as these will be killed too!

Chemical treatment
As the life cycle of whitefly is so rapid (eggs hatch to adults in as little as three weeks), a regular spraying regime will have to be followed. In order to control and then eradicate whitefly in all of its life stages there are a number of chemical pesticides available. These include formulations containing the chemicals bifenthrin and thiacloprid.

Aphids (*Aphidoidea*)

The aphid, the term for blackfly and greenfly, is probably the most likely harmful insect to be encountered by gardeners. These pests attack the

Sticky glue trap.

soft-growing tips of diverse garden plants in the spring and throughout the summer months. Aphids weaken the affected plants by sucking the sap from young, fresh growth. They then exude sticky honeydew-like fluid that adheres to whatever it falls upon and can also transmit diseases to their host plants. Aphids will cause a lot of damage if left unchecked. Auriculas are not often invaded by aphids but that is not to say that an attack is unlikely.

Non-chemical treatment
Sticky glue-traps as used against other pests will ensnare aphids quite well. You can also give the ladybirds in your garden a holiday by taking them into the greenhouse or frame where they will have a nice time devouring the aphids.

Another tried-and-tested method of aphid control is to place pots of French marigolds in the greenhouse, dotted amongst your auriculas. This method proves very effective and you will also have the added benefit of colour in the greenhouse when your auriculas have stopped flowering.

Chemical treatment
There are a number of insecticides that are very effective at destroying greenfly and other aphids. These are based on the chemical acetamiprid.

Woolly aphis *(Erisoma lanigerum)*

This pest is often only noticed when an attack is well

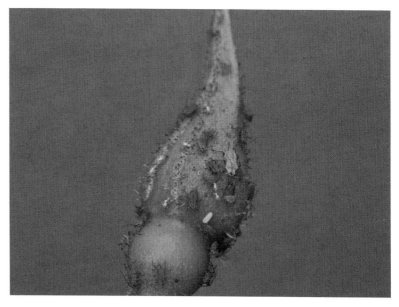

Aphid attack.

advanced. Woolly aphides tend to establish themselves around the neck and root of a plant and are observed as a woolly fluff covering the plant at compost level. It is not known why this insect attacks auriculas but one school of thought is

Ladybird on the prowl.

that plants that have become too dry may be susceptible to attack. Applications of systemic fungicides containing bifenthrin or imidacloprid will be effective against woolly aphis. Another method is to take the affected plants from their pots and paint over the site of the attack with methylated spirit.

Caterpillars

It is quite possible that caterpillars, which enjoy succulent young plant growth, may attack auriculas during the early part of the growing season. If they are seen, pick off the grubs and destroy them by squashing with your fingers, providing you are not too squeamish, or remove them from your plants and lay them on your lawn or bare earth and whistle to signal to the local birds to come and feast!

Slugs and snails (Gastropoda)

These pernicious pests are more of a problem where auriculas are planted outside in beds or borders than in greenhouses. The succulent auricula leaves are a tempting meal for foraging slugs or snails and these pests will have a good munch if they are hungry and auriculas happen to be in their way. An army of slugs will ravage a bed of alpine or border auriculas, and snails will not be put to shame by the slugs.

It is a sad fact that the British Isles is slug and snail heaven: our climate has cool and damp conditions in spring and early summer allied with

---

Controlling slugs and snails

- Copper bands placed around plants will deter slugs as they will receive an electric shock if they attempt to slide over.
- Grit, gravel or crushed shell placed around the plants act as an effective barrier as slugs and snails are not able to glide along to reach the plants.
- Hand-picking them off, if you are not too squeamish. After rainfall, when slugs seem to make an appearance en-masse, is a good time to do this. Slugs and snails have a homing instinct and so move them to at least 30m away.
- Yoghurt pots or jam jars a quarter filled with beer are effective traps. Sink them into the ground so that they stick out a small way above ground level. Slugs will climb in to enjoy an evening tipple, so give them a night they will never remember!
- Hollowed-out half lemons, oranges or marrows, strategically placed, are quite useful as slug and snail traps.
- Nematodes watered onto the soil in the garden can also be an effective way to rid the borders of slugs and snails.
- If you are lucky enough to own a large property with a pond, introduce ducks, which will do a simply marvellous job in keeping your garden free of slugs and snails.

---

mild winters enabling slugs and snails to thrive. They dwell in moist conditions and will lurk under lush and abundant foliage during cool and wet summers.

Non-chemical treatment
Good garden husbandry should be practised to prevent attacks by slugs and snails. As far as possible keep your beds, borders, greenhouses and frames free from weeds and detritus. Opened bags of compost and pieces of abandoned wood will attract slugs and snails. If bags are left in greenhouses, ensure the bag tops are secured with string; slugs and snails like the sweaty conditions of the moist plastic.

Chemical control
Slug pellets, which are made from the chemicals metaldehyde or methiocarb, are the main method for controlling these pests chemically. These small blue pellets should be put under pieces of wood or tile and placed near to the plants to be protected. Beware before resorting to this method of control as slug bait is thought to be harmful to other more pleasant wildlife, and domestic pets. There are a number of other options open to gardeners for controlling slugs and snails.

Woodlice (Oniscidea)

The woodlouse is not an important pest of auriculas as it tends to eat dead plant material. Nevertheless, other creatures will feed on woodlice so it is best to be free of this nibbler. They are generally more active during the night but can be seen scurrying around in the day on their way to damp places. Keep the greenhouse or frame free of dead plant material or disused

TOP LEFT: A snail in for a munch; **TOP RIGHT:** Woodlice; **CENTRE LEFT:** Yellow slug; **CENTRE RIGHT:** Small slug; **BOTTOM LEFT:** Banded snails; **BOTTOM RIGHT:** Auricula leaf virus.

pieces of wood, which is another favourite place for the woodlouse.

Sciarid flies *(Lycoriella auipila)*

Also known as fungus gnats, these midge-like creatures lay their eggs in the compost of potted plants and the resulting emergent maggots then feed on young roots and organic matter in the pots. As multi-purpose composts and peat substitute compost are practically pure organic matter, it is these composts that are more likely to get invaded than the loam-based John Innes composts.

Sciarid flies seldom attack auriculas in pots but outbreaks are not unknown so the grower should be ever vigilant. These small black fliers are generally noticed as they fly and hover above potted plants. More often than not this will occur during the warmer months of the year and when the greenhouse atmosphere is humid. Attacked plants are weakened and often become stunted. The fungus gnats' invasion allows entry points for root disease such as *Pythium*.

Control can be exercised by hanging yellow glue-traps over the pots or by the use of a synthetic pyrethroid concentrate containing the active ingredient permethrin.

DISEASES

Auricula viral leaf disease

This disease is manifested by streaks or blotches of a pale yellow colouration on the foliage of auriculas. The viral disease is not endemic and occurs only occasionally in auriculas and then mainly during the cooler months of the year. By observation it appears that only certain cultivars are affected by this virus, and the disease does not appear to transmit to other auriculas growing nearby.

Auricula viral disease may be present on the plants when they are introduced to a collection, so thorough examination prior to purchase, if possible, is very important.

By the time late winter and early spring has arrived then the virus is more often than not grown out by new foliage. No harm is done to the flowering performance, as the disease is confined to the foliage only. A virus outbreak is nevertheless an annoyance and it detracts from the auriculas' natural beauty, more than being a serious threat to a collection.

As always, observe good hygiene in the greenhouse or frame by removing old foliage from the plants and keeping the benches clear of detritus. Sterilize scalpels and knives to prevent inadvertently spreading the virus from plant to plant.

Botrytis cinerea

The fungal disease botrytis, or grey mould, is a fairly common disease that affects a wide range of plants including auriculas. It appears when damp, warm conditions are prevalent and air flow is restricted or non-existent. A bad attack, caused by very humid conditions, will be manifest by a fluffy grey or off-white mould growing on many parts of the plant. Conversely a low incidence of humidity may induce an attack, for some unknown reason, but the symptoms are not as severe.

This fungal disease thrives on wet plants and dead plant material, which is why it is vital to keep a clean greenhouse and practise good garden husbandry by clearing away old leaves and flower heads. To remove dead leaves keep the auricula plant steady by supporting it with one hand whilst gently pulling the dead leaf from the plant with the other. It is so easy to almost uproot a potted auricula when tugging away at old leaves.

The spores of botrytis can also invade wounds on live plants so it is important that care is taken when removing dead or dying leaves from auriculas. Botrytis has the ability to remain dormant in nascent plant tissues, emerging and causing rot at a later time.

Chlorosis

This abnormal condition is only encountered occasionally. Chlorosis turns the green colour of the stems and leaves to a pale green and yellow. This yellowing is due to a deficiency in the necessary quantities of green chlorophyll pigments and a deficiency in the essential elements of iron, magnesium or manganese. Most often it is a lack of the iron element that is the reason for chlorosis.

Iron can be locked up by too high a level of lime in the compost or soil and in severe cases death is more than likely for the affected plant. Plants that have reached this stage will have stopped photosynthesizing.

In order to prevent chlorosis occurring always use balanced compost, and not one that does not have a provenance. The absence of light, genetic factors or a viral infection may well also be causal influences.

To remedy the situation an application of sequestered iron will be needed to help rectify the deficiency. Always use it at the manufacturer's recommended rate of application.

Fasciation

This disorder is seldom met with and is more of a curiosity than a worry, but it is very annoying to have an auricula suffer this disease. The effect is observable by a coalescence of stems or flowers producing a flattened structure. It is not certain what causes this abnormality but it is thought that it could be as a result of damage to a plant's growing tip (apical meristem) by animal or man, or possibly by a bacterial infection.

Sooty mould *(Ascomycete)*

The disease sooty mould is generally caused by an attack of aphids. These pests exude a sticky substance

that becomes invaded by a black mould. A build-up of this mould will prevent the correct photosynthesis of the host plant. The blackened mould hardens as it ages but can be removed by careful washing of the affected foliage.

IN CONCLUSION

Vigilance is the keyword in order to identify, control and hopefully destroy attacks by pests and diseases. Check your auriculas daily and particularly before going away for a holiday. Get a trusted friend or relative to look over your auriculas regularly and ensure they are able to take remedial action if required whilst you are away.

Occurrences of attack by pests or diseases on auriculas are not all that common, but an attack can occur at any time so it is best to be prepared.

Things to Do Before Going Away

- It would be a wise step to ensure that your auriculas receive an application of vine weevil killer shortly before leaving for a holiday to deter an attack by vine weevils and/or aphids whilst you are away.
- Ensure there are sticky traps suspended over the tops of your plants.
- Always have a supply of your preferred chemical in stock ready for use if needed.
- Always practise good husbandry by being thorough and tidy.

Fasciation of auricula stalk.

6 The Alpine House

An alpine house – that is, a greenhouse designed or set up for the sole purpose of alpine plant culture and display – is one of the best ways to grow and show auriculas. It offers the plants a sheltered environment, whereas when planted in the garden, with the exception of the border and alpine types, the flowers are often ruined by inclement weather conditions. The mealed flowers and foliage of show auricula types in particular can be completely devastated by high winds and driving rain.

In their natural environment of the high Alps auriculas are protected for a part of the year by a covering of snow that effectively shields them from excessive rainfall, severe frosts and cold blustery winds during the winter months. An alpine house will provide an alternative form of protection needed in order to grow auriculas in the best conditions. As well as the *P. auricula*, the alpine house will provide protection for the primulas *allionii*, *marginata* and *vernales*. You could also grow, alongside auriculas or independently, *Cyclamen* species such as the *africanum*, *alpinum*, *elegans*, *coum*, *graecum*, *hederifolium*, *persicum* and others, along with plants such as *Erigeron*, *Hepatica*, *Saxifraga*, *Soldanella*

and *Lewisia*. These are a few among many alpine subjects that may be grown, shown and enjoyed in the alpine house.

FEATURES OF AN ALPINE HOUSE

Traditionally, the alpine house is an unheated greenhouse constructed of cedar wood and it usually sits on a wall of bricks or a concrete plinth. The extra height afforded by a base makes access and ease of working in it a lot better. Alternatively, it is constructed of timber or a brick wall up to around waist height. As there is less glass used in this construction than in a traditional greenhouse there is less fluctuation in temperature.

The siting of the alpine house

The alpine house needs to be sited carefully in the garden and preferably positioned north-to-south along its length. The ground will need to be flat, level and consolidated. It is possible to site an alpine house under a small-leaved deciduous tree, such as birch, to provide dappled shade in the summer months. This will negate the need for artificial shading, and full available light is maintained during the winter months after leaf fall.

Do not site the alpine house very close to tall hedges, fences or walls, as these will

cast a shadow for a part of the day if not all of it.

> ### Points to Consider for an Alpine Greenhouse
>
> * It will need a solid base of concrete or paving slabs to give stability and provide an internal path.
> * It will need a purpose-made wall of brick to give more headroom under the greenhouse frame.
> * It should have multiple roof vents if possible.
> * Louvered or traditional opening side vents are recommended to allow maximum ventilation.
> * Often the alpine house is divided in to two sections: a growing area and a display area. Both sections will need to have sturdy, waist-high benches along each side.

Flooring

The alpine house flooring should be concrete or better still made from paving slabs. This will make for easy maintenance: brush regularly to tidy up detritus and sprinkle on water in hot, dry summery weather to provide some humidity.

The paving flags should be laid on top of level concreting sand. A mixture of building sand and cement should be brushed into the joints and then watered. This will set and prevent weeds from entering the structure.

OPPOSITE PAGE:
Alpine auricula 'Larry'.

allows good air circulation. Quite often both forms of staging will have an under-shelf storage facility for pots and trays. This comes in very handy and is worth paying a little extra for.

Paving slab greenhouse floor.

Plunging

Some alpine enthusiasts sink their potted alpines into sand or a similar material in a purpose-made raised bed on top of the display bench. This process, known as plunging, can assist in three ways. The first is moisture equalization; second, it prevents the pots from freezing solid in severe frosts; and finally, it keeps the roots cooler in the summer.

The pots are inserted almost up to their rims in a layer of sharp sand that is kept moist; this helps the pots to retain water and so prevents them drying out. It is advisable to place a piece of nylon fabric, such as from a pair of tights, in the bottom of the pots in order to prevent compost loss from the drainage holes. Clay pots will dry out quicker owing to their porous nature so more watering will be needed if these are used.

During the winter months the pots will actually be kept drier by plunging, which is important for auriculas as they require to be kept drier at this time of the year. The sand will draw out excess water from the pot.

Plunging is usually carried out by a few dedicated alpine growers. More often than not alpine plants are free-standing on the benches.

Benches or staging

The benches in an alpine house are best installed at around waist height; any lower than this and you are going to struggle if you are prone to backache. If it is too wide then it becomes difficult to reach plants placed at the rear. Ideally the width should be from the sides of the structure reaching to the door jambs.

Staging or benches can be made quite easily from good-quality disused timber. However, if you prefer not to make your own there are several businesses specializing in selling greenhouse staging and benching. There are also benches made from aluminium available. Some of these have been designed with a surface that can be turned over to form a tray to hold gravel or capillary matting. You can also use slatted wooden staging, which

Heating

The alpine house will generally be unheated but some growers give a little heat at flowering time if the weather is particularly cold. Only in extremely prolonged freezing weather is a small paraffin stove or electric heater used to stop the pots from completely freezing, if so desired. This would be one of those rare occasions when the door would be closed, apart from when there are high winds or thick fog. If a paraffin stove is to be used, ensure that there is a little ventilation at all times through the windows to ensure correct operation of the heater unit.

Auto roof vent from the inside.

Ventilation

Follow an open door policy all year around except in the foulest of weather. All alpine plants require careful attention and plenty of fresh air throughout their growing season. During periods of close and foggy weather, the vents and doors should be closed in order to prevent the damp air from infiltrating the alpine house. Re-open as soon as these conditions have passed to allow full ventilation again.

A purpose-made alpine house will provide the airier conditions needed for good alpine plant growth. However, if you cannot afford an alpine house – and they are costly – then try and purchase a greenhouse with maximum ventilation facility. A conventional greenhouse will benefit from the temporary removal of some side panes

Auto roof vent from the outside.

of glass during the growing season. This will assist in air circulation but do take care if doing this that rain does not splash onto your plants. Also take care when handling glass as the edges of untoughened glass can be very sharp. Always wear gloves for this task.

Consider the purchase of a louvre kit for a conventional

greenhouse. These may be installed onto a timber or metal greenhouse by removing a pane of glass. Use the removed glass to act as the opening and closing blades by cutting to size with a glass cutting implement. Multiple roof vents and louvred side vents are not necessarily a prerequisite, but are desirable in order to achieve as much ventilation as possible. At least one roof vent or the greenhouse door left open all the year round and shut only in extremely hostile weather conditions is the bare minimum requirement for ventilation .

Roof vents can be fitted with automatic openers that work by using a wax-filled tube that expands or contracts according to temperature fluctuations. They are cheap to buy, very easy to install, slimline in construction and effective through a wide temperature range. Watch out, though, as auto vents will open in mild rainy weather and water drops may fall onto the plants below, which will spoil and possibly ruin them.

Shading

From late spring onwards put shading on the roof and sides of the alpine house to lessen the effect of brilliant sunshine. Not to have shading is a dangerous policy as the intensity of the sun through glass will cause the plants to dry out all too quickly and may also lead to scorching, especially if water is present on the foliage. Having gone to the expense and trouble of installing an alpine house, it would be foolish not to complete the job by considering the damage the intensity of the sun can cause during the summer months.

Liquid shading

The liquid method, using Liquid Coolglass™, will provide shading that lasts for one season from a single application. During brighter weather this shading becomes more intense, as the product is light sensitive and responds accordingly. Conversely, when conditions are duller the product allows more light transmission.

It is easy to apply, using a garden atomizing sprayer or a paintbrush that can be tied to the end of a stout cane to reach the uppermost parts of the greenhouse. It is very advisable to have shading in place during the summer months unless the alpine house is under a small leaved deciduous tree.

Fabric shading

Rolls of green netting made of ultra-violet-stabilized polyethylene, which are attached to the glass frames, provide around 50 per cent shade factor value. There are woven slits positioned closely on the fabric to provide secure anchor points by using plastic plugs and washers that attach to the inside of the greenhouse frame. The netting is usually guaranteed for a period of four or five years but is often effective longer than this. Using netting rather than a liquid is a cleaner way of applying shading.

Watering

The watering regime should be reduced from about the middle to the end of the autumn, which is when auricula growth slows right down before winter dormancy. During the winter watering will be necessary only once every three weeks or so. In mild winters some auriculas may carry on growing with no dormancy break whatsoever.

Alpine House Tips

- An all-glazed greenhouse could be fitted with rolls of bubble wrap for use in the winter to keep the severest of cold out.
- Collected and stored in vessels under the benches in the greenhouse, rainwater will be slightly warmer to use than water drawn off very cold from the water butt or tap. Taking the chill off the water this way is in no way detrimental to the plants.

Enjoy your alpine house. Keep it in tip-top condition and invite your friends and family in to admire your collection during the spring flowering season.

The alpine house also makes a fine a refuge from gardening weather and your least favourite domestic chore, especially if you can squeeze in a chair!

TYPES OF ALPINE HOUSE

A traditional alpine greenhouse

The traditional alpine greenhouse is preferably

mounted on a brick wall or stone plinth to allow a little more height and to help preserve the timber. Note that side vents as well as the usual roof vents allow maximum ventilation as needed by alpine subjects. The timber used in construction is western red cedar (*Thuja plicata*), which is a hard, straight-grained soft wood that has very good durability.

A small lean-to alpine greenhouse

The alpine glasshouse shown, which is an adaptation from a small vine house, is affixed to an exterior wall and has side and roof vents as well as louvred glass panes to afford maximum ventilation. The timber used in its construction is again western red cedar and the greenhouse features sheets of toughened glass.

An adapted greenhouse

A conventional greenhouse on a wall, such as the one illustrated, would benefit alpine subjects greatly if it had side ventilation. It would make a very good large alpine greenhouse if adapted this way. Note the staging installed at a workable height.

The alpine-style greenhouse shown here has timber sides up to the bench height, helping to conserve heat. It would need side louvres fitted to improve airflow.

A traditional alpine greenhouse.

Small lean-to greenhouse. (Photo: Gabriel Ash, Monument Farm, Farndon, Near Chester)

Greenhouse on a wall.

Greenhouse with minimal
ventilation.

A patio cold frame

This upright patio cold frame is an ideal small structure in which to grow and care for auriculas. It is manufactured in red cedar and allows maximum light and ventilation with its clever design. Its placement on paving flags near to a house ensures convenience.

A grand cold frame

The grand cold frame is also made from western red cedar. It has twin lids (lights) which can be propped opened using the stays provided. As well as housing auriculas it may also be used for many other gardening purposes.

An upright patio cold frame. (Photo: Gabriel Ash, Monument Farm, Farndon, Near Chester)

A grand cold frame. (Photo: Gabriel Ash, Monument Farm, Farndon, Near Chester)

7 How to Make an Auricula Theatre and a Cold Frame

A simple auricula theatre can be made quite easily with a minimum of skill and just a few basic woodworking hand tools. The easiest and most economical way to make one is by utilizing an old set of bookshelves. Old bookshelves are generally constructed of three or four shelves with sides, and they may have been free-standing or attached to a wall. It may well be that you have a disused set of bookshelves in the attic or garage. If not then you could always trawl the second-hand furniture stores or junk shops for a set.

If an unused set is not available, you can purchase timber for the purpose from your local timber merchant or DIY superstore; the cost of new timber is not as prohibitive as you might at first think. If you are making one from scratch then get your local timber merchants to price up the wood for you. If you consider it too expensive also check out the cost from a DIY store. More often than not the material from the timber merchant will be top quality, if you ask for such, and they will also cut the pieces to size, which will save you a lot of time.

Auricula theatres should preferably be situated and affixed to a north-facing or west-facing house wall. If

mounted facing towards the south and south-east the plants will dry more rapidly and possibly damage will be sustained to flower buds and flowers from the early morning sun.

MAKING AN AURICULA THEATRE FROM A BOOK SHELF UNIT

Materials and tools required

You will need:

- a set of unused bookshelves
- tongue-and-groove timber
- exterior-quality coloured wood preservative
- lead or mineral roofing felt
- a paintbrush
- medium-grade and fine-grade sandpaper
- a sandpaper block
- a crosscut handsaw or electric jigsaw
- sprigs or ½in (12mm) length nails
- a stout tack hammer
- breathing protection.

Method

- To provide protection from rainfall or snow the auricula theatre will require a roof. The top shelf can act as this. If the sides are above the top shelf carefully saw away these side pieces to leave them level with the top shelf, which will now become the roof.

- Put on appropriate safety protection (such as a dust mask and safety goggles) before the next stage.
- Rub down the sawn side pieces with medium-grade sandpaper and then with fine-grade sandpaper, with a sandpaper block wrapped inside the sheets
- Measure the rear of the bookshelves to provide a back; you can make one easily using good-quality tongue and groove timber.
- Sand down the tongue and groove and cut to size.
- Place the first length in the centre of the back and secure it to the back of the top shelf using sprigs or nails. Continue by working down the unit securing the back piece to to the back of the shelves, finishing on the bottom shelf.
- Add more tongue and groove, working outwards from the centre to the sides to complete the back.
- It is very likely that the tongue and groove end pieces will overlap the sides, in which case mark the overlap with a pencil and then saw away to make a snug fit. Sand down any rough edges.
- The last job will be to paint the whole unit, which is now your auricula theatre, using a waterproof preservative in a colour of your choice.

OPPOSITE PAGE:
Alpine auricula 'Piers Telford'.

HOW TO MAKE A NEW AURICULA THEATRE FROM SCRATCH

A purpose-made new auricula theatre can be made fairly easily and inexpensively at home, and requires only a few more tools than if you are converting an old set of bookshelves for the purpose. A new auricula theatre can be made to have three or four shelves, a tongue and groove or chipboard back, and a sloping roof protected with lead sheet to afford protection from rainfall. The whole structure must be painted with several coats of good-quality wood preservative, of a colour that enables the flowering auriculas to stand out. Generally a black backdrop or a dark green shade is most suitable. The use of a bottle green or black velvet curtain draped at the rear would add more authenticity. For the purpose of this example the construction of a three-shelved unit is described. It may be wall-mounted or free-standing.

The timber used is planed all round (PAR) redwood, also known as deal or Scot's pine. This wood is invariably available from your local timber merchant, who will cut the planks to the required sizes. Alternatively it may be bought unsawn from a DIY superstore for you to cut.

Materials and tools required

You will need (all dimensions are approximate):

- 2 × 40in (1020mm) × 6.5in (165mm) × ¾in (18mm) redwood, for the sides
- 3 × 24in (610mm) × 6.5in (165mm) × ¾in (18mm) redwood, for the three shelves
- 3 × 25¾in (655mm) × ¾in (18mm) × 8mm batten, for the pot retainers
- 1 × 27in (685mm) × 6¾in (172mm) × 6mm marine-quality plywood, for the roof
- 2 × 30in (762mm) × 6in (152mm) code 4 lead flashing, to cover the roof

- 7 × 39¾in (1010mm) tongue and groove, for the back
- ½in (12mm) sprigs or steel nails
- 18 × 1¼in (32mm) No. 6 Posidriv screws
- coloured exterior wood preservative
- waterproof wood glue
- general-purpose strong glue
- a small paintbrush
- a stout tack hammer
- a crosscut saw
- a power or hand drill and bit
- a countersink
- a bradawl
- a Posidriv-type screwdriver
- medium-grade and fine-grade sandpaper
- breathing protection
- sash clamps
- a square
- a pencil
- strong garden scissors or tin snips
- fine-grade steel wool
- patination oil.

Method

- In order to save time, have your local timber merchant cut the sides and shelves to the desired lengths, or mark the appropriate lengths using a pencil and square and carefully cut using a sharp handsaw or jigsaw with the appropriate blade.
- To obtain an angle for the roof the front of the side pieces need to be cut at a length of 39½in (1004mm), and the back to 40in (1020mm).
- Place the two side pieces flat together, ensuring they are

Cut wood for auricula theatre.

even at the top and bottom, and with a pencil mark all around both pieces where you want to position the shelves. The bottom shelf will need to be around ½in (12mm) from the bottom of the sides. This allows airflow through the bottom of the unit and provides more stability if the theatre is to be free-standing.

- Separate the sides and drill three holes, evenly spaced from the outsides of the side pieces. Countersink the outside of the holes.
- Insert the bradawl through the drilled holes, making pilot holes in the shelf ends on both sides.
- Screw the sides to the shelves after applying a thin length of waterproof glue to the shelf ends.
- Apply sash clamps, ensuring the unit is square. Leave overnight or for at least twelve hours before continuing.
- Nail onto the top of the sides the piece of marine-quality plywood that forms the roof, allowing for an overhang at the front.
- Nail the pot retainer pieces onto the front just above the shelves.
- Nail the tongue and groove back into place after applying wood glue to the tongues and sliding them together. Work from the centre of the back outwards.
- It is very likely that the tongue and groove end pieces will overlap the sides, in which case mark the overlap with a pencil and then saw the overlap away

them to make a snug fit. Sand down any rough edges.
- Wearing dust protection, sand the unit thoroughly with sandpaper before applying four coats of the wood preservative.
- The final job is to put on the lead roof. Cut the two lengths of lead using strong garden scissors or tin snips. Scalloping of the front edges on the lead, if desired, is purely for decoration. Either use a 5in (125mm) plant pot or a purpose-made template placed on the front edges of the lead strips. Draw around the pot or template with a pencil and cut away with the scissors or tin snips.
- Apply a layer of general-purpose glue to the underside of the rear lead strip. Place the cut lead strips to overlap onto the roof and attach to the sides using the sprigs or nails.

- The front edge will need to be folded in order to make a neat edge. Cut a small slit at the appropriate angle towards the corners of the roof. Fold the front piece around to the side and nail into place.
- Gently rub down the lead if it is not clean using fine-grade steel wool. Then rub all over with a soft cloth.
- Finally, apply patination oil to the lead roof as per the instructions on the can.

Auricula theatres may be used to display other plants such as herbs and summer-flowering house plants or foliage pot plants. Succulents such as the *Echeveria*, *Kalanchoe* and *Sempervivum* all make good subjects for display. Enjoy your auricula theatre.

The home made auricula theatre.

Succulents in the home made auricula theatre.

8 Showing Auriculas

Raising a show-worthy auricula from home-produced offsets is quite an achievement. The show winners are the auricula cultivars that have been nurtured, coddled and cosseted and grown as close to perfection as possible and will be deserving winners. Learning to raise one's own auricula cultivars by the techniques of hand pollination may be seen as a difficult challenge. To progress from there and to exhibit auriculas raised this way for the first time must surely be viewed as a test of growing skills and confidence, in allowing one's efforts to be judged and applauded, or not, by one's peers.

Growing auriculas well is a craft and, like all crafts, it takes time for proficiency to be achieved. But what better way to display these skills than by exhibiting one's prized plants at the auricula shows. This is the epitome of auricula cultivation for some and ensures that new varieties are regularly being produced in order to perpetuate auricula cultivation, hopefully ad infinitum.

There are many auricula enthusiasts who would not dream of exhibiting their plants but are more than happy to grow them for their own pleasure or for commercial considerations. Auriculas

are not difficult to grow but experience is needed to grow them well: housing, composts, pest and disease control or, better still, eradication, fertilization and watering all need to be on the mark in order to produce excellent plants that show well and have a chance of winning. Growing for showing is a simple matter of ensuring these criteria are met.

The goal is to produce auricula plants of compact and well-balanced proportions, with flat pips of bold colours. The foliage is important too, with the emphasis placed on clean and healthy leaves that preferably cover the top of plant pots and assist in hiding the compost. The auricula stems require being strong yet flexible and able to support the pips in a circular arrangement. Canes may be used to add rigidity and perpendicularity to the stems if necessary, and these are usually a split bamboo cane dyed green. Some growers use wooden barbeque skewers, which are perfectly acceptable. Whichever is used, the end to be inserted into the plant pot will need to be sharpened using a pencil sharpener, in order to prevent damage to the roots of the auriculas, and cut to a length that suits the particular truss. The cane is then tied to the stalk using green-coloured knitting wool and a wad of cotton wool if needed to add further protection to the flower truss when in transit.

SHOW REQUIREMENTS

The exhibited plants should be pest and disease free and compact in overall size with preferably one rosette of leaves covering the top of the pot. The stems and footstalks should be strong yet pliable.

The pips are required to be uniform in dimension. Overcrowding of pips can cause a problem and thinning out will be required in order to present plants that display a truss of pips that just touch each other. The alpines, doubles, edges, fancies, selfs and striped all require a minimum of five pips per truss as standard. The size of the individual pips follows a traditional standard that is 29mm for the alpines, doubles, selfs and stripes, 32mm for the edges and between 29mm and 32mm for the fancies.

NB Border auriculas are shown for effect only and are not subject to the standards of Florists' Auriculas.

The standards for the edges

- The pips need to be, as far as possible, flat and formed in a circular shape and the individual flower petals should be evenly sized and notch-free.
- The tube, in the centre of the pip, should be of a round nature, smooth-edged and a golden colour or pure deep yellow.

- The pollen-bearing anthers should be placed regularly around the tube, circularly arranged, and a golden or pure deep yellow colour. They should not protrude over the top of the tube. They should curve in towards each other and be positioned above the stigma (thrum-eyed). This is very important as if the stigma is positioned over the stamens (pin-eyed) then the auricula will be disqualified.
- The circle of paste should be smooth, pure white, dense and free from any imperfections.
- The body colour or ground colour (preferably black) should be of a circular nature and feather into the edge colour a little but not extend to the outer point of the edge.
- The green edge should be free from meal (farina) and evenly coloured. The grey edge requires an even coating of meal that allows for the green to show as a grey effect. The meal of the white edge should completely obscure the green colour of the petals. In all cases the meal should be even and of a bright white nature and free from blemishes.

The desirable characteristics of show plants are exacting, as can be seen. But with careful cultivation a lot if not all of these requirements can be met with not too great a difficulty. There is an element of fortune too, but the standards are there for a purpose and the exhibiting grower should strive to achieve these.

The standards for the selfs

- The selfs, of one colour only, should be clear and pure in colour: unshaded, free from veining and having a velvety texture. The pips are to be rounded and free from notches.
- They should have a smaller tube than the edges and the circle of paste should be smooth, pure white, dense and free from imperfections.

- The anthers should be a rich yellow colour and be placed regularly around the tube.

The selfs, of course, are of one clear colour only and the pip itself should be smaller at around 29mm, as opposed to the edges whose optimum diameter is 32mm. The beauty of the selfs more than makes up for their more diminutive pip size. The range of colours is wide and with the contrast of the paste (the dense farina) they look very attractive.

The standards for the doubles

- The standards for the doubles are in general the same as for the show cultivars, in that they should have a minimum of five pips.
- The pips must be circular in nature and offer two full rows of petals as a minimum requirement. This is necessary in order to obscure the tube completely.
- The petal edges should, as far as possible, be free from notches.

The quantity of petals on the doubles varies from cultivar to cultivar. However, it is important that the number of petals is enough to fully cover the tube and fill the pip. Open-centred doubles will be disqualified. The petals may be shaded or self-coloured.

The standards for the alpines

- The standards for the alpines are in general the

SHOWING AURICULAS **135**

same as those of the show types.

- Both gold-centred and light-centred alpine auriculas are admissible to the shows.
- There should be a minimum of five pips.
- The eye of gold-centred alpine auriculas should be a bright gold colour, be free from blemishes and an even shade. The eye of the light-centred alpine auriculas should be a white or light cream colour and, as with the gold-centred alpines, be blemish-free.
- All of the pips should be of a velvety nature and intensely coloured.
- The flower and the foliage should be devoid of any meal.
- The tube must be rounded and the same colour as the eye.
- The petals should be a uniform colour, be free of notches and should shade uniformly from the darker colour next to the eye to a paler hue at the edge of the outermost point of the petals.

The alpines are, along with the borders, undoubtedly the easiest of auriculas to grow. They are far easier to obtain and make an ideal beginner's auricula. That is not to say that the alpines are in any way inferior to the show types. Indeed, the alpine class is always a popular one for showing. The many cultivars of exquisite colouring and shading give a lot of joy to gardeners, exhibitors and visitors to the shows.

The standards for the stripes

- The standards for the stripes are in general the same as for those of the other show types.
- The pips must be flat and round in shape. The optimum size is 29mm.
- A golden or rich yellow tube is necessary.
- The stripes, either of farina or colours, should spread outwards from the circle of paste, radiating to the outermost point of the petals. They should be clear and evenly spread.

The striped auriculas hold their own well at the shows and this class is growing in popularity once more after years of being in the doldrums.

The standards for the fancies

- General standards for this class apply.
- The pips should be between 29mm and 32mm in size.
- The fancies are judged on overall appearance.

SHOW DETAILS

National Auricula and Primula Society Show Dates

The main show dates for the National Auricula and Primula Societies (NAPS) are as follows.

NAPS Northern Section

- The main show is usually held during the first

Tools Needed for Showing

There are a few tools and bits and pieces needed to take to the shows to present your auriculas in the best way:

- new or restored pot plant labels for each and every auricula you are showing
- a pencil and/or permanent marker pen
- tweezers
- green-dyed wool
- cotton wool
- cotton wool buds
- split canes or plastic-covered stiff wire
- a scalpel or very sharp pair of manicure scissors
- a camel hair brush
- a moistened cloth for wiping the pots
- a notebook, for ideas and contact names and numbers
- a box (a plastic tool box works well) to carry them all in.

weekend in May each year at Kingsway School, High Grove Road, Cheadle nr. Stockport, Cheshire, SK8 1NP.

NAPS Midlands and West Section

- The major Midland Auricula Show takes place during April each year at Arden School, Station Road, Knowle, Solihull, West Midlands, B93 0PT.

NAPS Southern Section

- The Auricula Show is held during the latter half of April at The Old Barn Hall, Church Road, Great Bookham, Surrey, KT23 3PQ.
- The West of England Auricula and Primula Show is held

during April each year at Saltford Hall, Wedmore Road, Saltford nr. Bath, BS31 3BY.

- The Saltwell Park Show is held over the two days of a weekend in April. The venue is Saltwell Park, Gateshead, Tyne and Wear, NE8 1HH.
- The Newbottle Show is held during May at the Newbottle Workingmens' Club, Front Street, Newbottle, Houghton Le Spring, Tyne and Wear, DH4 4EP.

General flower shows with classes for auriculas

- The Ancient Society of York Florists' Spring Show is held in April each year at the Conference Hall, Askham Bryan College, Askham Bryan, York, YO23 3FR.
- The Harrogate Spring Flower Show is held over four days in mid-to-late April each year at The Great Yorkshire Showground, Harrogate, North Yorkshire, HG2 8PW.

Other shows

- The West Midland Group Auricula Show is held in April at the Uplands Allotments, Handsworth, West Midlands, B21 8EX.
- The Malvern Spring Gardening Show is held at The Three Counties Showground, Malvern, Worcestershire, WR13 6NW. The show is held during May of every year; several Auricula nurseries display and sell plants and sundries over four days.

Conclusion

It is hoped that you as an aspiring or experienced auricula grower have found this book useful and informative. I have taken you through a brief history of auriculas and their cultivation in the British Isles and Europe. Advice has been given on simple growing techniques and the breeding of new cultivars of this wonderful alpine flower. A comprehensive list of cultivars, of which the majority are available from specialist auricula nurseries, is also included. There has also been discussion of pest and disease control, alpine houses, auricula theatres and showing standards.

Down the centuries we have been blessed in the British Isles with some remarkable pioneering gardeners and plant hunters who have brought us, the gardening public, myriad new plants, intricate garden plans, scenic landscapes and treasured gardens. This has helped turn us into a land of gardeners and garden lovers and auricula culture remains a significant part of this.

Recent years have seen a renewed surge of interest in auricula culture and many more new varieties have been produced since the end of the Second World War and continue to be bred today. A handful of dedicated growers are working on new production, particularly of the stripes and doubles, and many enthusiastic amateurs are still keenly hybridizing alpines and show types.

Some older auricula cultivars were in danger of dying out, but with the modern processes of micropropagation some have been saved and are flourishing once again. Whatever one's thoughts on this method of propagation it must be said that without it we auricula lovers would be denied the beauty and form of those that have been saved. It has not all been plain sailing, however; there have been problems with this form of culture with some progeny not growing true to form.

This test-tube horticulture has and will continue to play an important role in horticulture in general – although in auricula culture perhaps only a small part. The simplicity of propagation of auriculas by way of offsets is to be encouraged among new growers, as is hand pollination as and when they are ready to tackle this most absorbing and rewarding of auricula culture techniques.

Well, what of the future? We are seeing now a resurgence of interest in gardening, albeit mainly in the 'Grow Your Own' sector, and sales of garden furniture and other gardening accoutrements are doing well. Alongside this sales of ornamental plants are steadily increasing too. Garden centres will sometimes sell trays of mixed alpine auricula and border auricula plants in the spring. This is a way for the novice to begin the auricular-growing experience, but for

the named cultivars and show types purchase from specialist nurseries is the way forward.

The beauty of auriculas has been and continues to be an attraction for many people. Renowned artists of an earlier age depicted some beautiful cultivars on magnificent canvases, although unfortunately most of these are in private collections. Spin-offs have appeared in the more recent past, with pictures of auriculas appearing on tapestries, playing cards, tableware, postcards and so on.

National Auricula Society membership levels are holding up well. The subscription fees are low, and you certainly get your money's worth with very informative and interesting articles published in the yearbooks and newsletters. If the resurgence in popularity of gardening continues, then membership levels of all garden societies should start to increase.

There are a handful of nurseries specializing in auriculas, located in England, Wales, Scotland and Ireland, all offering the more familiar cultivars and also some of the show types. Keen amateur auricula growers often sell their surplus rooted offsets through Internet auction sites. It is hoped that this method of trade will, over time, draw attention to auricula growing and help with raising the profile of auriculas with the gardening public.

Appendix: Auricula Cultivars

AURICULA CULTIVARS FROM THE PAST

The following is a list of auriculas that were grown during seventeenth and eighteenth centuries. The cultivars listed here are a mixture of popular green, grey and white edges and selfs grown during that time.

Alderman Parsons
Alexander Magnus
Ancient Lady
Archer's Champion (of England)
Ashton's Man of War
Ashton's Prince of Wales
Ashworth's Rule All
Atcherley's Alpine Shepherdess
Barlow's King
Barlow's Morning Star
Bearless's Superb
Beesley's New Metropolitan
Berry's Lord Primate
Bishop of Lichfield
Borth's Freedom
Bright Phoebus
Brook's Dreadnought
Brown's Mrs Clarke
Buckley's Jolly Tar
Butterworth's Duchess of Wellington
Butterworth's Lord Hood
Cheetham's Countess of Wilton
Chilcott's Brilliant
Chilcott's King
Clapton Hero
Clegg's Black and Green
Clegg's Crucifix
Clegg's Lady of Honour
Clegg's Sovereign
Clough's Defiance
Clough's Dolittle
Clough's Jingling Johnny

Cockup's Eclipse
Cockup's Wortley Comet
Colonel Wortley Conspicua
Commander in Chief
Cox's British Hero
Cox's Pillar of Beauty
Danae
Darlington's Lord Nelson
Dean's Regulator
Dean's Smoker
Dickinson's Matchless
Doctor Syntax
Done's Rule All
Double Painted Lady
Duke of Beaufort
Duke of St Albans
Duke of Wellington
Dyson's Queen
Earl Grey
Eaton's Volunteer
Egerton's Lord Combermere
Eggleton's Alexander
Emmerton's Favourite
Fair Helena
Faulkner's Hannibal
Faulkner's Manchester Hero
Faulkner's Ne plus Ultra
Fieldhouses Fair Rosamund
Findley's Purple of Tyre
Fletcher's Mary Ann
Foden's Rosamund
Foden's Victory
Galloway's Glory of Oldham
Glory of Bolton
Glory of the East
Glory of Maidenhead
Goldham's Vertumnus
Gorton's Champion of England
Gorton's Goldfinch
Gorton's Grand Turk
Gorton's Stadtholder
Grand Presence
Grime's Flora Flag
Grime's Hyder Ali
Grime's Privateer
Harrison's William Pitt

Hayley's Prince of Wales
Hedge's Brittania
Hepworth's Robin Hood
Hero of the Nile
Heye's Lovely Ann
Hinche's Lily of the Valley
Hoffey's Lord Nelson
Honour and Glory
Hopkin's Mine of Gold
Hortaine
Howard's Lord Nelson
Howard's Sweepstake
Hufton's Squire Mundy
Hughe's Liberty
Hughes's Pillar of Beauty
Jewel of Holland
Kent's Queen Victoria
Kenyon's Free Brittania
Kenyon's Ringleader
Kenyon's Surprise
Kettlesby's True Blue
King of the Alps
Lady Darby
Lawrie's Field Marshall
Lawrie's Glory of Cheshunt
Lee's Colonel Taylor
Lee's Lord Lee
Lee's Sir William Wallace
Lee's Talavera
Lee's Venus
Lightbody's Fair Flora
Lightbody's Star of Bethlehem
Litton's Imperator
Lord Lascelles
Madder's Brilliant
Major Cartwright
Mellor's Fair Lady
Mellor's Lord Howe
Mellor's Reform
Metcalfe's Hero
Metcalfe's Lancashire Hero
Moore's Jubilee
Moore's Marchioness of Salisbury
Mount Pleasant
Oddie's Queen Caroline

Oddie's Rest
Ogden's Sir Rowland Hill
Ollier's Lady Anne Wilbraham
Owen's Princess of Wales
Page's Champion
Page's Duchess of Oldenburg
Page's Waterloo
Parke's Black Joke
Partington's Sir Solomon
Partington's Trafalgar
Partington's Violet
Pearson's Bajadoz
Pearson's Liberty
Pollitt's Highland Boy
Pollitt's Highland Laddie
Pollitt's Ruler of England
Pollitt's Standard of England
Pollitt's Woodland Laddie
Pope's Cardinal
Pope's Gardener
Pope's Lady Dartmouth
Popplewell's Conqueror
Porter's King
Porter's Queen
Pott's British Champion
Pott's Delegate
Pott's Eclipse
Pott's Regulator
President
Princess Elizabeth
Queen of May
Queen Victoria
Ray's Jupiter
Redmayne's Metropolitan
Redstar
Reform
Ridding's Junius
Rider's Sovereign
Rider's Waterloo
Rising Sun

Rone's Farmer
Royal Purple
Royal Widow
Rule Arbiter
Scholes's Mango
Scholes's Mrs Clarke
Shakespeare
Sim's Jessie
Simpson's Commander
Simpson's Marquis of Granby
Sir Charles Wager
Sir Sidney Smith
Slater's Cheshire Hero
Smiling Beauty
Smith's Duke of Sussex
Smith's Emperor
Smith's Waterloo
Snook's Beauty
Snook's Regulator
Squire Mundy
Stretch's Alexander
Syke's Complete
Taylor's Alexander
Taylor's Glory
Taylor's Incomparable
Taylor's Ploughboy
Taylor's Princess Royal
Taylor's Victory
The Bishop
Thompson's Bang Up
Thompson's Revenge
Thornicroft's Invincible
Tranter's Constellation
Vett's King
Victoria
Warris's Collosus
Warris's General Butcher
Warris's Union
Waterhouses Seedling
Whitacker's Rule All

Whitacker's True Blue
Whitehead's Reform
Wild's Black & Clear
Wild's Colonel Anson
Wild's Highland Lass
Wild's Lord Bridport
Williamson's Brittania
Wood's Delight
Wood's Lord Lascelles
Woodman's Ethiopian
Woodman's Lord Burlington
Wrigley's Northern Hero
Yates's Collingwood
Yates's Morris Green Hero
Zisca

ALPINE AURICULA CULTIVARS

A majority of the following alpine auricula cultivars are available currently from the auricular-growing nurseries, although there are some that are now quite rare and difficult to obtain. The first column shows the cultivar name, next is the date that the particular cultivar was either first bred or introduced. The breeder's name follows and then the colour, and finally the type of alpine auricular – either gold-centred (GC) or light-centred (LC). I have tried to be as accurate as possible with the details, unfortunately there are some gaps where certain details are unknown.

Name	Year	Breeder	Colour	Type
Abundance		D. Hadfield	Pink/red	GC
Achates	1993	D. Telford	Pink	LC
Admiral			Purple	LC
Adrian	1970	A. Delbridge	Lilac/purple	LC
Adrienne Ruanne	1992	M. Ruanne	Brown	GC
Aga Khan		J. Douglas	Red/black	GC
Agamemnon	1993	D. Telford	Pink	LC
Alamo	1991	D.Telford	Pink	LC
Alan	1953	F. Faulkner	Crimson	GC
Alan Ravenscroft			Brown/gold	GC
Alexandra Georgina			Light purple	LC
Alf	1980	L. Bailey	Red	GC
Alfred Charles			Lavender/purple	LC
Alicia			Purple	LC
Alison Jane			Purple	LC
Alison Telford			Red	GC
Allensford		Fieldhouse Nursery	Brown	GC
Amethyst			Brown	GC
Amicable	1994	D. Telford	Brown	GC
Ancient Order	1994	D. Telford	Brown	GC
Ancient Society	1997	K. Bowser	Orange/brown	GC
Andrea Julie		D. Telford	Orange/brown	GC
Andrew Hunter	1972	D. Telford	Red/brown	GC
Andy Cole	1990	D. Telford	Pink	LC
Anne Taylor	1993	D. Taylor	Pink	LC
Anwar Sadat	1978	R. Taylor	Pink	LC
Applecross	1968	D. Edwards	Crimson	GC
Arabian Night	1995	D.Telford	Lavender blue	LC
Arapaho			Brown/gold	GC
Arctic Fox	1991	D. Telford	Lavender blue	LC
Argus	1887	J.J. Keen	Plum red	GC
Arlene	1984	L. Rollason	Pink	LC
Arthur Delbridge	1984	D. Telford	Deep pink	LC
Arwen	2002	J. Radford	Red	GC
Ashcliffe Gem	1988	C. Timpson	Pink	LC
Ashcliffe Gold	1984	C. Timpson	Gold/brown	GC
Aurora	1962	J. Douglas	Pink	LC
Austin	1993	D. Telford	Purple	LC
Autumn Fire	1988	C. Timpson	Red	GC
Avril Hunter	1988	D. Telford	Light Blue	LC
Bacchus	1971	A. Delbridge	Wine	GC
Barr Beacon	1998	Les Allen	Red	GC
Basuto	1995	J. Douglas	Red	GC
Beatrice	1914	J. Douglas	Blue	LC

Name	Year	Breeder	Colour	Type
Beckminster	1989	Gwen Baker	Red/brown	GC
Bewitched	1990	D. Telford	Brown	GC
Bilbo Baggins	1999	J. Radford	Brown	GC
Blossom	1970	Mrs. S. E. Auker	Red shades	GC
Blue Bonnet	1936	J. Douglas	Purple	LC
Blue Heaven	1992	D. Telford	Pinky blue	LC
Blue Lace	2000	Les Allen	Dark blue	LC
Blue Yodeler	2001	K. Bowser	Blue	LC
Bob Dingley	1992	D. Telford	Lavender	LC
Bolero	1964	C.F. Hill	Coppery Red	GC
Bookham Firefly	1936	J. Douglas	Red/brown	GC
Boromir	1999	J. Radford	Pink	LC
Bournebrook	2002	P. Redfern	Dark pink	LC
Bradford City	1996	S. Cravens	Dark red	GC
Brazos River	1995	D.Telford	Dark pink	
Breckland Joy	2001	Les Allen	Pink shades	LC
Brenda's Choice	1987	A. Delbridge	Plum	LC
Bright Eyes	1983	D. Telford	Brown	GC
Broad Gold		House of Douglas	Brown	GC
Brown Ben	1993	H. Cohen	Brown/gold	GC
Brown Bess	1993	H. Cohen	Brown	GC
Bubbles	1979	D. Telford	Brown/red	GC
Buccaneer	1992	D. Telford	Red	GC
Bunty			Red	GC
Buoyance	2003	Les Allen	Gold	GC
Butterwick		D. Salt	Brown	GC
Cambodunum	1996	D. Telford	Purple	LC
Cameo	1964	C.F. Hill	Red/gold	GC
Caramel	1994	C. Timpson	Brown	GC
Carioca	1998	D. Telford	Red	GC
Carole	1977	K. Ellerton	Brown	GC
Carreras	1992	D. Telford	Red	GC
Cartouche	1992	D. Telford	Brown	GC
Carzon			Brown	GC
C.F. Hill		D. Salt	Brown/red	GC
Charlie's Aunt	1992	D. Telford	Red	GC
Chelsea Bridge			Blue/purple blue	LC
Cheops	1997	D. Telford	Purple	LC
Cherry Picker	1994	D. Telford	Pink	LC
Chocolate Soldier		D. Telford	Brown	GC
Choir Boy		Les Allen	Blue/pink	LC
Cicero	1985	L. Kaye	Pink	LC
Cindy		D.Telford	Brown	GC
Ciribiribin	1998	D. Telford	Pink	LC

Name	Year	Breeder	Colour	Type
Cobden Meadows	1985	M. Sheader	Purple	LC
Connaught Court	1995	D. Telford	Dark pink	LC
Conquistador	2002	Les Allen	Brown	GC
Coppi	2002	P. Bowen	Deep purple	LC
Craig Vaughn		D. Telford		LC
Cranbourne			Deep purple	LC
Crecy	1995	D. Telford	Pink	LC
Cuddles	1994	D. Telford	Brown	GC
C.W. Needham	1934	Percy Johnson	Deep purple	LC
Daniel	1996	D. Telford	Blue/purple	LC
Daniel T. Taylor		J. Radford	Gold	GC
Del Boy		Les Allen		GC
Dianne		W. Hecker	Wine	GC
Dilemma	2000	K. Bowser	Red	GC
Dill	1996	K. Leeming	Plum	LC
Divint Dunch	1990	D. Telford	Plum/purple	GC
Don Head	1996	A. James	Pink	LC
Doreen Stephens	1989	D. Telford	Red	GC
Doris Jean	1975	F. Jacques	Pink	GC
Douglas	2002	D.Telford	Dark blue	LC
Douglas Bader	1995	D. Telford	Deep and pale blue	LC
Drax	1998	T. Nicholls	Pale brown	GC
Dubari		L. Kaye	Lavender	LC
Dusky Girl	1996	Les Allen	Plum/brown	GC
Dusky Maiden	1987	A. Delbridge	Brown/purple	GC
Eastern Promise	1995	D. Telford	Orange-red/brown	GC
Ed Spivey			Purple	LC
Eddy Gordon	1995	D. Telford	Red	GC
Edinburgh	1998	Les Allen	Blue	LC
Edith Allen			Red	GC
E.G. Linton	1995	D. Telford	Deep pink	LC
Elf Star			Blue	
Eli Jenkins		P. Bowen	Brown	GC
Elizabeth Ann	1974	J. Sherwood	Red	GC
Ellen Thompson	1961	J. Robinson	Blue	LC
Elsie		J. Allen	Brown	GC
Elsie May	1972	D. Telford	Purple	LC
Elsie Swinbourne		D. Telford	Red	GC
Emmett Smith			Red	GC
Endeavour	1998	T. Mitchell	Brown	GC
Enlightened	1990	D. Telford	Pink	LC
Eric Price			Orange	GC
Erica	1984	Gwen Baker	Red	GC
Eve Guest	1970	A. Hawkes	Blue	LC

Name	Year	Breeder	Colour	Type
Eye Opener	1970	D. Telford	Pink	LC
Fairy	1930s	J. Douglas	Pink/purple	LC
Falariki		K. Leeming	Plum	LC
Fandancer			Pink	LC
Fergus			Pink	LC
Ferrybridge		D. Skinner	Blue	LC
Finchfield	1976	Gwen Baker	Light brown	GC
Firenze	1992	D. Telford	Red/pink	GC
First Lady	1990	Les Allen	Brown/orange	GC
Forge	1957	F. Faulkner	Crimson	GC
Foxfire	1999	Les Allen	Red	GC
Fradley	1988	C. Timpson	Red	GC
Frank Crossland	1930	C. Faulkner	Blue	LC
Frank Faulkner	1951	F. Faulkner	Red	GC
Frank Jennings	1995	D. Telford	Red	GC
Fred Livesey	1994	Les Allen	Purple	LC
Fresco	1994	D. Telford	Brown	GC
Gail Atkinson		T. Atkinson	Brown	GC
Galen	1970	R. Cole	Red	GC
Gary Pallister		K. Leemimg	Brown	GC
Gay Crusader	1982	L. Kaye	Pink	LC
Gazza	1996	D. Telford	Pink	LC
Gee Cross	1980	J. Gibson	Red	GC
Generosity		M. Newberry	Red/orange	GC
Geordie	1991	D. Telford	Purple	LC
George Jennings	1995	D. Telford	Pink	LC
Gimli	2004	J. Radford		
G.L. Taylor	1994	D. Telford	Dark Pink	LC
Gold Seam	1995	D. Telford	Brown/yellow	GC
Golden Boy	1995	D. Telford	Brown	GC
Golden Eagle	1991	D. Telford	Brown	GC
Golden Gleam			Brown	GC
Golden Glory			Gold/bronze	GC
Golden Harvest			Yellow/gold	GC
Golden Wedding	1998	C. Timpson	Brown	GC
Goldthorn	1976	Gwen Baker	Gold/brown	GC
Goldwin	1980	A. Hawkes	Gold/brown	GC
Gollum	1988	J. Radford	Orange	GC
Good Report	1992	D. Telford	Blue	LC
Gordon Douglas	1918	J. Douglas	Blue	LC
Gorey	1992	D. Telford	Purple	LC
Gwen		A. Hawkes	Purple	LC
Gwenda	1998	C. Timpson	Blue	LC
Gypsy		House of Douglas	Purple	LC

Name	Year	Breeder	Colour	Type
Gypsy Rose Lee	1993	D. Telford	Brown	GC
Habanera	1989	D. Telford	Purple/pink	LC
Hallmark	1996	Les Allen	Pink	LC
Hamari		Les Allen		
Harry Hotspur	1992	D.Telford	Purple	LC
Haughmond	1978		Brown/orange	GC
Hazel		L. Rollason	Deep Purple	LC
Heady	1994	D. Telford	Pink	LC
Heart of Gold	1995	D. Telford	Gold	GC
Hebers	1994	D. Telford	Gold	GC
Hermia		House of Douglas	Lavender	LC
Highland Park	1902	K. Bowser	Blue	LC
Hughie	2001	D. Telford	Brown	GC
Hill House		D. Telford	Dark Pink	LC
Howard Telford	1994	D. Telford	Blue	LC
Ian Greville		C.Timpson	Pink	LC
Ibis	1960s	House of Douglas	Pink	LC
Ice Maiden	1995	D. Telford	Blue	LC
Ida			Blue	LC
Immaculate	1993	D. Telford	Gold	GC
Impassioned	1993	D. Telford	Red	GC
Impeccable				
Imperturbable		D. Telford	Red	GC
Indian Love Call	1993	D. Telford	Gold/red	GC
Iris Scott	1995	D. Telford	Purple	LC
Isabella	1998	J. Titcombe	Pink	LC
Jack Dean	1981	L. Bailey	Purple	LC
Jack Redfern	2002	P. Redfern	Lavender	LC
Jaffa	2000	Les Allen	Orange	GC
Janie Hill	1959	C. F. Hill	Brown	GC
Jean Fielder	1970	A. Hawkes	Pink	LC
Jean Jacques	2001	D.Telford	Red	GC
Jeannie Telford	1977	D. Telford	Dark pink	LC
Jenny	1968	W. Elliot	Red	GC
Jersey Bounce	1998	D. Telford	Orange/brown	GC
Jessie Holland		S. Popple	Pink	LC
Jessie Lightfoot	2001	P. Bowen	Brown	GC
Joan Elliot		Joe Elliot		
Joanna Shaylor		J. Eddington	Purple	LC
Joanne	1971	J. Bell	Blue	LC
Joe Perks	1993	D. Telford	Brown	GC
John Gledhill			Red	GC
John Leech			Red	GC
John Stuart		W.G. Elliot	Plum/wine	GC

Name	Year	Breeder	Colour	Type
John Wayne	1977	L. Bailey	Pink	LC
Jonathon	1997	T. Mitchell	Lavender	LC
Joy	1931	P. Johnson	Purple	LC
Joyce		M. Rossiter	Deep blue	LC
June	1960	S. Edwards	Lavender	LC
Jura		G. Douglas	Brown	GC
Just Steven	2000	T. Mitchell	Blue	LC
Karen McDonald	1995	D. Telford	Lavender	LC
Katchachurian	1992	D. Telford	Red	GC
Kelso	1930	J. Douglas	Purple	LC
Ken Chilton	1995	D. Telford	Purple	LC
Ken Gailton	1995	D. Telford	Plum	LC
Kerkup	1968	D. Telford	Pink	LC
Kevin Keegan	1983	D. Telford	Deep pink	LC
Key West	1996	P. Bowen	Dark pink	LC
Kilby	2004	J. Eddington	Dark pink	LC
Kim	1972	A. Stubbs	Brown	GC
Kimberworth Boy	2001	J. Eddington	Pink	LC
Kingcup	1944	C. Haysom	Red	GC
Kingfisher	1997	D. Telford	Pink	LC
Kintail	1930	House of Douglas	Dark blue	LC
Kohinoor	1996	D. Telford	Dark pink	LC
Lady Daresbury	1931	C. Faulkner	Pink	LC
Lady Drury			Pink/blue	LC
Lady Joyful		A. Hawkes	Pink	LC
Lady of the Vale	1988	C. Timpson	Brown	GC
Landy	1987	D. Telford	Brown	GC
Langley Park	1992	D. Telford	Purple	LC
Laphroaigh		D. Telford	Brown	GC
Lara	1993	D. Telford	Blue	LC
Laredo	1998	D. Telford	Red	GC
Largo	1969	A. Hawkes	Brown	GC
Larry	1995	D. Telford	Blue	LC
Lazy River		D. Telford	Red	GC
Lee	1994	D. Telford	Purple	LC
Lee Clarke	1995	D. Telford	Pink	LC
Lee Paul	1990	D. Telford	Maroon or Brown	GC
Lee Sharpe		K. Leeming	Gold/brown	GC
Legolas	2000	J. Radford	Plum	LC
Leroy Brown	2001	D. Telford	Brown	GC
Lewis Telford	1990	D. Telford	Red	GC
Light Hearted	1994	D. Telford	Blue	LC
Lila	1999	D. Telford	Purple	LC
Lilac Domino	1993	D. Telford	Pink	LC

Name	Year	Breeder	Colour	Type
Lilian Hill	1968	C.F. Hill	Lavender	LC
Limelight	1995	D. Telford	Lavender	LC
Linda	2000	C. Timpson	Blue	LC
Ling		L. Kaye	Red	GC
Lisa	1979	D. Telford	Pink	LC
Lizzie Files	2004	C. Timpson	Brown	GC
Lothlorien	2000	J. Radford	Pink	LC
Lynn	1980	A. Delbridge	Pink	LC
Mahmoud	1993	L. Kaye	Gold	GC
Mandarin	1992	D. Telford	Pink	LC
Margaret Faulkner	1953	F. Faulkner	Purple to crimson	LC
Margaret Irene	1995	D. Telford	Pink	LC
Margot Fonteyn		D. Telford	Brown	GC
Marion Howard Spring	1974	J. Ballard	Red/pink	GC
Mark		D. Telford	Pink	LC
Martha Livesey	1994	Les Allen	Pink	LC
Martha's Choice	1998	Les Allen	Pink	LC
Maureen Millward	1974	A. Millward	Brown	GC
May	1996	A. Delbridge	Pale pink	LC
Meadowlark	1993	D. Telford	Blue	LC
Melifluous	1990	D. Telford	Pink	LC
Merridale	1976	Gwen Baker	Gold	GC
Mesquite	1998	D. Telford	Orange/red	GC
Metha	1993	D. Telford	Pink	LC
Mexicano	1996	Les Allen	Orange	GC
Mick	1989	D. Telford	Brown	GC
Milkmaid	1931	J. Douglas	Blue	LC
Millicent	1985	R. Barter	Blue	LC
Mink	1974	J. Ballard	Red	GC
Mirabella Bay	1995	D. Telford	Pink	LC
Mirandinha	1991	D. Telford	Red	GC
Miriam	1977	J. Allen	Purple	LC
Miss Newman	1997	S. Popple	Deep purple	LC
Mollie Langford		G. Dawson	Purple	LC
Monarch			Purple	LC
Monica	1975	K. Wharton	Purple	LC
Monks Eleigh		Tim Coop	Orange	GC
Moonriver	1996	D. Telford	Purple	LC
Mrs L. Hearn	1930's	J. Douglas	Blue	LC
Mrs R. Bolton			Purple	LC
Murray Lanes	1994	D. Telford	Purple	LC
My Fair Lady	1996	D. Telford	Deep purple	LC
Myrtle Park	1990	D. Telford	Brown	GC
Nefertiti	1996	D. Telford	Purple	LC

Name	Year	Breeder	Colour	Type
Nessun Dorma	1994	D. Telford	Pink	LC
Newsboy		Les Allen	Pink	LC
Newton Harcourt		J. Sewell	Pink	LC
Nickity	1988	C. Timpson	Brown	GC
Nicola Jane	2000	K. Leeming	Blue	LC
Nina	1999	Les Allen	Lavender	LC
Nonchalence	1991	D. Telford	Pink	LC
Norma	1978	K. Ellerton	Pink	LC
Old Smokey	1991	D. Telford	Brown	GC
Olton	1963	F. Edwards	Gold	GC
Opus One		D. Telford	Pink	LC
Ossett Sapphire	2000s	T. Mitchell	Pale blue	LC
Otto Dix	2000	P. Bowen	Brown	GC
Overdale	1962	K. Gould	Red	GC
Paddlin Madeliene	1995	D. Telford	Red	GC
Paleface	1993	D. Telford	Pink	LC
Paragon	1952	H. Burbridge	Pink	LC
Pastiche	1991	D. Telford	Brown	GC
Paula			Pink	LC
Pauline	1998	P. Bowen	Purple	LC
Pavarotti	1994	D. Telford	Dark pink	LC
Peggy	1937	C. Faulkner	Blue shades	LC
Peggy's Lad	1991	L. Rollason	Pink	LC
Pequod		D. Hadfield	Purple	LC
Peter Beardsley	1989	D. Telford	Orange/red	GC
Pharoh	1994	D. Telford	Brown	GC
Phyllis Douglas	1908	J. Douglas	Purple	LC
Pierot		D. Hadfield	Purple	LC
Piers Telford	1991	D. Telford	Brown	LC
Pimroagh		D. Telford	Purple	LC
Pink Lady		House of Douglas	Pink	LC
Pinkie		K. Leeming	Pink	LC
Pippin	1931	J. Douglas	Red shades	GC
Pixie	1976	A. Delbridge	Pink	LC
Playboy	1999	Les Allen	Dark pink	LC
Polestar	1997	D. Telford	Purple	LC
Pretender		D. Telford	Red	GC
Prince John	1916	J. Douglas	Maroon	GC
Purple Emperor			Purple	LC
Quintessence		D. Telford	Pink	LC
Rab C. Nesbit		D. Telford	Orange/brown	GC
Rabley Heath	1972	A. Hawkes	Deep blues	LC
Rachel	1995	Les Allen	Pink	LC
Radiant	1930s	J. Douglas	Gold	GC

Name	Year	Breeder	Colour	Type
Rameses	1992	D. Telford	Purple	LC
Red Mark			Red	GC
Redcar		G. Douglas	Dark pink	LC
Regency		L. Rollason	Red	GC
Rene		J. Ballard	Red	GC
Respectable	2000	Les Allen	Brown	GC
Richard Shaw			Red	GC
Risdene	2000	C. Timpson	Golden brown	GC
Rivendell	1999	J. Radford	Orange	GC
R.L. Bowes	1989	D. Telford	Brown	GC
Robert Lee	1993	D. Telford	Purple	LC
Rodeo	1960	C.F. Hill	Brown	GC
Rosalie		M. Sheader	Pink	LC
Rose Kaye			Crimson to pink	GC
Rothesey Robin	1996	Les Allen	Pink	LC
Rowena		J. Stant	Pale pink	LC
Roxborough	1913	House of Douglas	Violet	LC
Roy Keane	1994	K. Leeming	Brown	GC
Ryecroft		Fieldhouse Nursery	Plum	LC
Sabrina	1999	Les Allen	Pink	LC
Saginaw		D. Telford	Pink	LC
Saint Elmo	1970	A. Hawkes	Orange/pink	GC
Salerno Crimson	2000	K. Leeming	Red	GC
Sam Gamgee	2002	J. Radford	Pink	LC
Sam Hunter		D. Telford	Red	GC
Samantha	2000	D. Telford	Pink	LC
San Gabriel	1999	Les Allen	Pink	LC
Sandhills	1989	A. Delbridge	Maroon	GC
Sandra	1973	H. Cohen	Plum	LC
Sandra's Lass	1986	L. Rollason	Pink	LC
Sandwood Bay	1971	D. Edwards	Red	GC
Sasha Files	2002	C. Timpson	Pink	LC
Shergold	1979	A. Hawkes	Brown	GC
Shotley	1976	D. Telford	Red	GC
Sidney	1992	D. Telford	Pink	LC
Sir John	1986	A. Hawkes	Red	GC
Sir John Hall		D. Telford		
Sirbol		K. Bowser	Orange	GC
Sirius	1979	F. Jacques	Maroon/cream	GC
Skylark	1992	D. Telford	Purple	LC
Slim Whitman	2004	K. Bowser	Brown	GC
Snooty Fox	1978	D. Telford	Brown	GC
Snooty Fox II	1982	D. Telford	Brown	GC
Soncy Face	1992	D. Telford	Pink	LC

Name	Year	Breeder	Colour	Type
Sonny Boy	1995	D. Telford	Orange/red	GC
Sophie		K. Bowser	Pink	LC
Sparky	1995	D. Telford	Dark pink	LC
Stella North	2003	D. Skinner	Pink/purple	LC
Stella South		D. Skinner	Pale purple	LC
Stoke Poges		G. Baker	Pink	LC
Stormin' Norman		D. Telford	Red	GC
Stuart West	1973	G. Elliot	Pink	LC
Subliminal		D. Telford	Red	GC
Sue		W. Elliot	Purple	LC
Sue Douglas		W. Elliot	Pink	LC
Sultan		G. Douglas	Gold	GC
Summer Sky		J. Douglas	Blue	LC
Summer Wine	1995	D. Telford	Wine	GC
Sumo	1993	D. Telford	Gold	GC
Susan			Blue	LC
Sweet Georgia Brown	1992	D. Telford	Brown	GC
Symphony	1990	A. Delbridge	Lavender	LC
T.A. Hadfield	1993	D. Telford	Red/pink	GC
Tally Ho	1959	C.F. Hill	Red	GC
Tarantella	1979	D. Telford	Red	GC
Ted Gibbs	1986	K. Bowser	Pink	LC
Ted Roberts	1977	J. Allen	Red	GC
Temerairie	1992	C. Timpson	Blue	LC
Terpo	1995	Les Allen	Red	GC
The Czar		D. Telford	Purple	LC
The Egyptian	1995	D. Telford	Red	GC
The Hobbit	1999	J. Radford	Brown	GC
The Lady Galadriel	2003	J. Radford	Purple	LC
The Sneep		D. Telford	Brown	GC
Thebes	1995	D. Telford	Pink	LC
Thetis	1906	J. Douglas	Purple	LC
Thutmoses	1993	D. Telford	Purple	LC
Toffee Crisp	1998	K. Bowser	Brown/orange	GC
Troy Aykman	1995	D. Telford	Red	GC
Tumbledown		D. Telford	Red	GC
Tummel		D. Telford	Brown	GC
Typhoon	1991	A. Delbridge	Brown	GC
Uncle Arthur		Tim Coop	Brown	GC
Unforgettable		D. Telford	Red/brown	GC
Valerie	1969	A. Hawkes	Purple	LC
Valerie Clare	1987	D. Telford	Brown	GC
Venitian	1993	D. Telford	Pink	LC
Vee Too	1967	A. Hawkes	Purple blue	LC

Name	Year	Breeder	Colour	Type
Venus	1989	Les Allen	Lavender	LC
Vera	2004	K. Bowser	Red	GC
Verdi	1943	H. Lennie	Brown	GC
Victoria de Weymiss	1979	D. Telford	Blue	LC
Victoria Park	1998	K. Leeming	Blue	LC
Vulcan	1955	F. Faulkner	Purple	LC
Walton	1957	G. Douglas	Blue	LC
Waltz Time	1991	D. Telford	Purple	LC
White Water	1993	D. Telford	Blue	LC
Whopee	1997	D. Telford	Pink	LC
Wichita Falls	1998	D. Telford	Pink	LC
Wide Awake	1990	D. Telford	Pink	LC
Wilf Booth	1994	D. Telford	Orange/brown	GC
Winifrid	1960	F. Faulkner	Red	GC
Winlation		D. Telford	Gold	GC
Woodmill	1985	M. Sheader	Pink	LC
Wookey Hole		D. Telford	Orange/red	GC
Yellow Ribbon		G. Manders	Brown	GC
Y.I. Hinney	1990	D. Telford	Violet	LC
Yitzhak Rabin		D. Telford	Orange/brown	GC
Zöe		House of Douglas	Orange/brown	GC

BORDER AURICULA CULTIVARS

There are far fewer border auricula cultivars in existence than there are alpine cultivars. The popularity is not now as strong as it once was. At one time, in the not too distant past, they were commonly planted in cottage and small town gardens, but today they do not enjoy the same regard as the alpines and the show types. This is a pity as the borders are very worthy auriculas and give great flowering displays. The flowers are in some instances not quite as exquisite as for the other types, but what they lose in beauty they more than make up for in garden and greenhouse flowering performance.

Name	Breeder	Colour
Alison Rose		Pink
Angela Gould		Purple
Apple Blossom		Pink/lavender
Aubergine		Purple
Bailey Boy		
Belgravia gold		Deep gold
Bellamy Pride	B. Walker	White
Bethan McSparron		
Bewerley's White		White
B.H. Peach		Peach
Bill Bailey		Orange
Bingley Folk		White

Name	Breeder	Colour
Blue Bella		Blue
Blue Haze		Blue
Blue Velvet		Blue and small white eye
Blue Wave		Lovely blue
Border Bandit		Orange
Border Patrol		
Bramley Rose		Wine
Bran		Almost black
Broadwell Gold	J. Elliot	Golden yellow
Brownie	S. Cravens	Orange/brown
Brownie Guider		
Bush Baby		
Ceri Nicole		
Chamois	J. Mercer	Yellow frilled petals
Charles Rennie		Pale pink
Cooper's Gold		Gold
Craig Dhu		Red
Curry Blend	I. Hawthorn	Curry powder colour
Dales Red	S. Cravens	Bright red
Dartagnon		
Dick Rodgers		
Doctor Lennon's White		White pale yellow
Duke of Edinburgh		
Dusky		Brown
Dusky Yellow		Yellow/brown
Dusty Miller		Yellow
Eden Alexander		Purple/blue
Eden Blue Star		Blue
Eden David		Purple
Eden Goldfinch		Yellow
Eden Lilac Time		Lilac
Eden Moonlight	B. Bach	Pale yellow
Emma Elizabeth		Pink
Frittenden Yellow		Bright yellow
Fullers Red		Red
George Harrison		White tinged with pink
George Swinford's Leathercoat	Ruth Duthie	Buff/brown/pink
Gnome		
Grandad's Favourite		Rose pink
Harlequin		
Jean Walker		
Johann Bach		Purple
Judith		
Julie Nuttall		Light purple

Name	Breeder	Colour
Kate Haywood		Pale yellow
Lavender Lady	A.M. Horseman	Lavender blue
Lambert's Gold		Gold
Lemon Sherbert		Lemon
Linnet		Mustard
Lintz	Lawrence Wigley	Velvet brown
Lockyer's Gem	S. Cravens	Pale yellow
Lucy Lockett		Yellow
MacWatt's Blue	Doctor MacWatt	Violet blue
Magnolia	Stella Coop	Creamy white
Mrs Cairn's Blue		Blue
Mrs Harris		
Mrs Lowry		
Mustard Sauce		
My Friend	Gill Dawson	Golden yellow
My Ode Boots		
Nancy Dalgety		
Oikos		Lavender blue
Old Clove Red		Rich deep red
Old Cottage Blue		Lilac and blue shades
Old Dublin Blue		Blue and Purple shades
Old Irish Blue		Lavender blue
Old Irish Green		Green edged
Old Irish Scented		Yellow and frilled edges
Old Mustard		Mustard
Old Red Dusty Miller		Red
Old Suffolk Bronze		Bronzy pink
Old White Dusty Miller		White
Old Yellow Dusty Miller		Pale yellow serrated blooms
Osbourne Green		Purple/green/cream
Our Pat		
Paradise Yellow		Yellow
Pink Hint		Pale pink
Pinkie Dawn		Dark pink
Proctor's Yellow		Mid-yellow
Purple Royale		
Queen Alexandra		Orange-yellow
Ralph's Tan		
Red Ensign		Red
Reddown First Swallow		
Reddown Rainman		
Reddown Yellow Ochre		
Redstart		
Robbo		Terracotta

Name	Breeder	Colour
Royal Velvet		Crimson/purple
Ruby Hyde		Ruby red
Rufus		Brick red
Rusty Red		
Shenstone		
Silas		Yellow
Sonia Nicolle		Purple/slate
Southport		
Starling		
Swiss Royal Velvet		
Tall Purple Dusty Miller		
Tawny Owl		
The General		Red
Winward Blue		Pale blue
Woodlands Lilac		
Wycliffe Harmony		
Wycliffe Midnight		Dark blue

DOUBLE AURICULA CULTIVARS

The double auricula cultivars, rather like the borders, have traditionally been fewer in numbers. The pollination of the doubles is trickier but has been perfected by a few dedicated florists over the past few years so more cultivars are gradually appearing. The double auricula displays a beauty of its own and there is little to match it in the world of double flowers.

Name	Year	Breeder	Colour
Abridge	1999	Les Allen	White
Albert Bailey	1988	L. Bailey	Mustard/orange
Albury	1972	W. Hecker	Purple
Alloway	1999	Les Allen	
Almond	1999	Les Allen	
Angostura			Dark plum
Ann Hyatt	1992	M. Ruan	Yellow/pink
Anne Swinthinbank		G. Ritchie	Yellow
Aquarius			Lavender cream
Arctic Fox			Purple
Ashwood Gold		Ashwood Nursery	Deep yellow
Audacity	1999	Les Allen	Brown
Avon Buster			Yellow
Avon Carrier			Peach
Avon Castle			Red
Avon Citronella		Pops Plants	Yellow
Avon Eclipse			Deep red

Name	Year	Breeder	Colour
Avon Elegance			Yellow
Avon Khaki		Pops Plants	Mustard
Avon Twist		Pops Plants	
Avon Valley			Apricot brown
Aztec		K. Wharton	Lime/gold
Bacchante		K. Wharton	Wine red
Baltic Amber		M. Sheader	Mustard
Barberry	1999	Les Allen	Purple Blue
Barnhaven Crème		J. Peters	Cream
Barnhaven Crème Violet		J. Peters	Cream/violet
Baroque		K. Wharton	Deep gold
Bella			
Bill Bailey			
Black Diamond			
Black Jack		M. Ruan	Dark red
Blackberry Way	2002	D. Tilt	Purple
Blackcurrant			Purple
Blakeney		D. Salt	Purple
Blue Bonnet	1938	J. Douglas	Purple
Blue Frills		Tim Coop	Blue
Bokay	1999	Les Allen	
Bonafide	1999	Les Allen	Yellow
Bonny Blue	2001	Les Allen	Blue
Brazen Hussey	1999	Les Allen	Brown/gold
Brimstone and Treacle	1991	L. Guest	Dark red
Buttermere		K. Wharton	Yellow
Cadiz Bay	1999	Les Allen	Burgundy/red
Calypso		K. Wharton	Pale orange
Camelot	1967	A. Hawkes	Purple
Cameo Beauty	1994	K. Wharton	Creamy yellow
Camilla	1970s	H. Wood	Purple
Capella	1999	Les Allen	Yellow
Cardinal Red			Red
Carmel	2001	K. Wharton	Pale brown
Catherine	1961	K. Gould	Yellow
Chantilly Cream	1980	Gwen Baker	Cream
Charles Bronson		L. Bailey	Brown
Charlotte Brooke		R. Dee	
Checkmate			Red
Chelsea Girl	2003	Lockyer	Blue
Chiquita	1997	K. Wharton	Orange/gold
Cinnamon		L. Bailey	Russet
Clatter Ha	1990	Ashwood	Purple
Claxby Plus Acre		D. Salt	

Name	Year	Breeder	Colour
Cloverdale	1999	Les Allen	Pale yellow
Cooks Hill	2003	R. Dee	
Cornish Cream			Pale yellow
Corrie Files	1988	C. Timpson	Blood red
Crimson Glow		K. Wharton	Deep red
Daisy Bank Charm	2001	K. Wharton	
Dark Eyes	1989	Les Allen	Deep purple
David Beckham	1996	K. Leeming	Lilac
Dedham	1999	Les Allen	
Delilah	1989	Gwen Baker	Purple
Denna Snuffer		M. Smith	Yellow
Devon Cream		D. Salt	Yellow
Diamond	1999	Gwen Baker	White
Digit	1992	K. Wharton	Gold
Digby		D. Salt	Purple
Dolly Vinny		G. Bach	Cream
Donn	2002	H. Pratley	
Dorado		M. Sheader	Yellow
Doublet	1975	A. Hawkes	Pink/purple
Doublure	1980	A. Hawkes	Purple
Doyen	1982	Gwen Baker	Dark red
Dusky Girl	1999	Les Allen	
Early Surprise			Pink
Edith Major		Fieldhouse	Pink/white
Elara			Yellow
Emberglow		M. Sheader	Orange/red
Emily P.		USA	
Ethel Wilkes		R. Dee	
Europa	2002	D. Tilt	Pale yellow
Excalibur	1988	Les Allen	Dusky pink
Falstaff	1988	Les Allen	Lavender/pink
Fantasia		K. Whaton	Red/white
Fiddler's Green		C. Hebdon	
Figurine		Les Allen	Pale pink
Firecracker	1996	K. Leeming	Red
Firsby		D. Salt	
Fishtoft	1980	D. Salt	Lavender
Fitzroy			Red/brown picotee
Forest Bordeaux			Plum red
Forest Burgandy			Wine
Forest Cappuchino			Pale coffee
Forest Duet			Purple
Forest Fire			Red
Forest Lemon			Pale yellow

Name	Year	Breeder	Colour
Forest Shade			Pink/peach
Forest Sunlight			Golden yellow
Forest Twilight			Purple
Frank Bailey		L. Bailey	Gold
Fred Booley	1999	D. Salt	Light purple
Friskney		D. Salt	Dark red
Funny Valentine		E. Picken	Red/purple
Gaia	1996	M. Sheader	Yellow
Ganymede		M. Sheader	Yellow
Gild Double			Yellow
Gill Baker		M. Ruan	
Gold Seal	1996	K. Ward	Gold/orange
Golden Chartreuse	1970	L. Bailey	Gold
Golden Hind	1993	K. Wharton	Gold/brown
Golden Splendour	1987	G. Black	Old gold
Grand Slam		K. Wharton	
Greswolde		L. Bailey	
Gwen Baker	1988	D. Salt	Yellow
Halo		D. Tilt	
Havannah		K. Wharton	Brown
Helena Dean		L. Bailey	Pale yellow
Helene	2000	M. Sheader	
Hereford	1999	Les Allen	
Hoghton Gem	1996	D. Cornforth	Golden yellow
Honey	1995	K. Leeming	Pale yellow
Hopley's Coffee		Hopley's Nursery	Light coffee
Illona			Cream
Inferno		D. Tilt	Red
Jayne Myers	1976	L. Bailey	Primrose
Joan Curtis		Pops Plants	Apricot
Joanne		D. Salt	Red
Jungfrau	1980s	D. Salt	Red
Kentucky Blue		R. Dee	Blue
Kirklands	1991		Purple/maroon
Lady day		L. Picken	Dark blue
Laguna	1996		
Lamplugh		B. Smith	Red
Lancelot	1996	Les Allen	Dark pink
Laura Woodhead		Pops Plants	
Lester		L. Picken	Blue
Leverton	1989	D. Salt	Lavender
Lichfield	1988	C. Timpson	Dark pink
Light Music	1999	Les Allen	Lavender
Lightmoor			Coffee

Name	Year	Breeder	Colour
Lima	1989	K. Wharton	Yellow
Lincoln Biscuit		D. Salt	Light coffee
Lincoln Bullion		D. Salt	Gold
Lincoln Butterscotch		D. Salt	
Lincoln Charm		D. Salt	Pink
Lincoln Chestnut		D Salt	Brown
Lincoln Consort		D. Salt	Burgundy
Lincoln Elf		D. Salt	Chocolate
Lincoln Fair		D. Salt	
Lincoln Foxy		D. Salt	Dark orange
Lincoln Glow		D. Salt	Yellow
Lincoln Halo		D. Salt	Orange /yellow
Lincoln Harmony		D. Salt	Orange
Lincoln Hazel		D. Salt	Orange/yellow
Lincoln Imp	1996	D.Salt	Pale yellow/red
Lincoln Imperial		D. Salt	Purple
Lincoln Lady		D. Salt	Primrose
Lincoln Major		D. Salt	
Lincoln Pippin		D. Salt	Deep orange
Lincoln Pirate		D. Salt	Burgundy
Lincoln Sparkler		D. Salt	Lemon
Lincoln Spice		D. Salt	Orange
Lincoln Whisper		D. Salt	Deep purple
Little Rosetta	1980	B. Smith	Reddish brown and yellow centre
Louisa Woolhead			Plum/pink
Madelaine Palmer		M. Ruan	
Maid Marion	1963	K. Gould	Yellow
Mardi Gras	1999	R. Dee	Dark red
Margery Thompson			Pink
Margo	1999	Les Allen	
Marie Crousse		D. Salt	Purple
Mary	1961	K. Gould	Yellow
Matchless	2000	Les Allen	Pale yellow
Matthew Yates	1980	L. Bailey	Deep purple
May Booley		D. Salt	Pink
Medallion	2001	K. Wharton	Gold
Megan	1992	L. Bailey	Brown
Mermaid		B. Smith	Red
Metis	2000	D. Tilt	Lavender purple
Mipsy Miranda	1996	H. Wood	Pale yellow
Mish Mish			Brown
Miss Bluey		D. Salt	Blue
Miss Pinky		D. Salt	Pink
Moonshadow		D. Salt	Yellow

Name	Year	Breeder	Colour
Moonshine		D. Tilt	Yellow
Moonstone	1978	Gwen Baker	Pale yellow
Mr Bojangles	1994	L. Picken	Yellow/pink
Nick Drake		R. Dee	Lavender blue
Nigel	1961	K. Gould	Violet
Nita	1994	D. Salt	Cream/mauve
Nona		D. Salt	
Nymph		K. Wharton	Cream
Nymphlike	2000	Les Allen	Cream
Olivia		M. Sheader	
Ophir		Les Allen	
Our Pat			Amethyst
Passing Cloud		R. Dee	White
Pat Rooney		M. Ruan	
Pauline Taylor		D. Taylor	
Pegasus		M. Sheader	Red
Peter Hall			Yellow
Phantom		T. Davies	Blue
Phaphos		K. Leeming	Wine
Piglet		D. Salt	Pink
Pink Fondant	1979	T. Coop	Pink
Pinkerton	2002	R. Dee	Pink
Plum Pudding			Dark plum
Pop's Blue			Blue
Porcelain		Les Allen	White/pink
Powder Paint	1999	R. Dee	Pink
Prima	1998	D. Tilt	Yellow
Prometheus		M. Sheader	Red
Purple Glow	1990	Gwen Baker	Purple
Purple Heart		H. Wood	Deep purple
Purple Lovely	2006	D. Salt	Purple
Purple Mermaid		D. Salt	Purple
Purple Rose	2006	D. Tilt	Purple
Quatford		E. Picken	
Quatro		Gwen Baker	Purple
Rebecca Baker	2006	M. Ruan	
Rebecca Hyatt			
Red Diamond	2000	Les Allen	Red
Requiem	2000	Les Allen	Deep purple
Reverie		Gwen Baker	Purple
Reynardine		E. Picken	Dark red
Riatty		B. Smith	Purple
Robinette			Red
Ronny Johnson	1996	K. Leeming	Cream

Name	Year	Breeder	Colour
Rose Conjou	1999	M. Sheade	Purple
Rosewood			Red/brown
Ruffles	1997	W.N. Millman	
Sarah Gisby	1997	K. Wharton	Dark red
Sarah Grey		D. Tilt	
Sarah Humphries	1992	M. Ruan	Purple
Sarah Lodge	1975	R. Cole	Rose pink
Satin Doll		E. Pickin	Deep lavender
Sea Lavender		K. Leeming	
Sea Mist	1976	A. Delbridge	Pale lavender
Shalford	1975	W. Hecker	Purple
Sibsey	1989	D. Salt	Blue
Silmaril		M. Sheader	Pale green/white
Sir Robert	1959	Lester Smith	Pink
Snow Maiden		R. Lee	White
Snowhite		D. Salt	White
Somersby		D. Salt	Yellow
Sophie	2002	M. Ruan	
South Barrow	1962	K. Gould	Red purple
Standish	1970	A. Guest	
Stella Coop		K. Leeming	Pink
Stripey		D. Salt	Lavender white
Stromboli	2001	D. Salt	Bright red
Sue Ritchie			Purple shades
Sundowner		R. Dee	Yellow/gold
Sunmaiden		K. Wharton	Yellow
Susannah	1960	A. Hawkes	Pink
Sword		D. Salt	Green/red
Tamar Gold	1997	W.N. Millman	Gold
Tango	1994	W.N. Millman	Lavender
Teawell Pride	1997	E. Pickin	Purple
Telesco		M. Sheader	
Terracotta		D. Salt	Red
The Cardinal			Deep red
The President	2000	Les Allen	Purple
Thirlmere	1984	Gwen Baker	Lavender
Thunderstorm	1996	L. Pickin	Dark red
Tim	200	K. Leeming	
Titania	1995	M. Sheader	
Top Affair		Les Allen	Yellow
Top Cat			
Top Man			
Treasure Chest		K. Wharton	Gold
Trident	1999	Les Allen	

Name	Year	Breeder	Colour
Trouble	1988	D. Salt	Coffee
Tupelo Honey		E. Pickin	Gold
Ushba		K. Wharton	
Vesuvius		D. Salt	Red
Walton Heath	1979	Ken Gould	Blue
Wanda's Moonlight	1999	Les Allen	Yellow
William Gunn		R. Dee	Brown
Windway Pisces	1985	Bernard Smith	Dark red
Winkle		D. Salt	
Wizard		D. Salt	
Wrangle	1992	D. Salt	
Zambia	1965	K. Gould	Dark red
Zircon		M. Sheader	

EDGED AURICULA CULTIVARS

The edged show auriculas could be described as the aristocrats of the auricula-growing world. They comprise some of the most exquisite flowers one is ever likely to come across. The place to see edged auriculas in all their glory is at the primula and auricula shows held during the spring. Dedicated growers vie to win the top prizes so you can be sure the specimens will be as perfect as they possibly can be.

The green edges

Name	Year	Breeder	Name	Year	Breeder
Agamemnon	2006		Flemminghouse	1967	J. Stant
Basilio		D. Hadfield	Forest Pines		
Beechen Green	1970	L. Wigley	Geldersome Green	1993	R. Taylor
Benny Green	2000	B. Coop	Gild green		
Bob Lancashire	1984	Jack Wemyss-Cooke	Glencoe		G. Douglas
			Gleneagles		G. Douglas
Bucks Green			Glenluce		G. Douglas
Carl Andrew		A. Chadwick	Green Jacket		
Cherubino			Green Magic		
Chloé	1957	F. Buckley	Green Mouse	1974	S. Kos
Chloris		F. Buckley	Green Parrot		
Clipper		B. Taylor	Greenheart		F. Buckley
Commando		A. Chadwick	Greenways		
Daphnis	2004	F. Buckley	Gretna Green		F. Buckley
Doctor Duthie	1975	P. Ward	Gruener Veltliner	1992	R. Taylor
Dorothy	1970	J. Ballard	Gwen Gaulthier		
Emerald	1962	D. Hadfield	Haffner	1974	D. Hadfield
Enigma		D. Hadfield	Hew Dalrymple	1947	C. Haysom
Envy			Holyrood		House of Douglas
Figaro	1985	D. Hadfield	Jack Wood	1983	D. Hadfield

Name	Year	Breeder	Name	Year	Breeder
John	1962	R. Newton	Roberto		R. Newton
Jorvik	2003	T. Coop	Sappho		D. Hadfield
Jupiter	1976	D. Hadfield	Scipio		D. Hadfield
Kingcraig	1976	L. Rollason	Serenity	1957	J. Ballard
Lincoln Green		D. Salt	Shirley Hibberd		
Linze II		D. Hadfield	Superb		
Mansell's Green		House of Douglas	Tamino		D. Hadfield
Marmion	1900	House of Douglas	The Maverick		
Mere Green	1997	Les Allen	The Wrekin		E. Pickin
Moselle		R. Taylor	Tinkerbell	1932	C. Cookson
Oban		G. Douglas	Tye Lee Green		Mrs Tye
Orb	1970	Doctor Duthie	Verity		B. Taylor
Pamino		D. Hadfield	Vivian	1932	S. Kos
Paris	1978	D. Hadfield	Walter Lomas		
Perdito	2001	K. Wharton	Water Willow		K. Wharton
Prague		D. Hadfield	Zephyr		
Prosperine	2001	K. Wharton	Zircon		D. Hadfield
Psyche		K. Wharton	Zodiac	1976	D. Hadfield
Robert Green		Les Allen	Zöe	2006	

The grey and white edges

The grey-edged and white-edged auriculas comprise some of the loveliest auriculas in existence. Along with their sisters the green edges they can look particularly beautiful and are grown to the limit of perfectionism.

Name	Year	Breeder	Name	Year	Breeder
Almonbury	1969	J. Stent	Cortez Silver		Les Allen
Arctic Fox		T. Coop	Douglas White		G. Douglas
Ascot Gavotte		T. Coop	Dovedale	1980	A. Delbridge
Athene	1996	D. Hadfield	Duchess of Malfi		Jack Wemyss-Cooke
Aviemore		House of Douglas			
Ben Lawer	1982	G. Douglas	Edith Mather		
Ben Wyves	1981	G. Douglas	Elegance		F. Buckley
Brian's Grey		B. Coop	Embley		C.G. Haysom
Brookfield	1979	P. Ward	Emery Down	1966	C.G. Haysom
Butternut		D. Hadfield	Falcon	1980	G. Douglas
Candida	1972	W. Hecker	Falsefields		
C.G. Haysom	1962	R. Loake	Freya	2006	S. Popple
Chebdon		C. Hebdon	Galatea		D. Hadfield
Cherille			Gavin Ward	1976	P. Ward
Clare	1980	P. Ward	Grabley		
Colbury	1955	C. G. Haysom	Grey Bonnet		
Cornmeal	1999	C. Y. Happy	Grey Dawn		
Corporal Jones	2000	R. Taylor	Grey Friar		F. Buckley

Name	Year	Breeder	Name	Year	Breeder
Grey Hawk	1988	D. Hadfield	Rosalie Edwards	1969	H. Hall
Grey Lag	1969	J. Ballard	S.D.Ward	1975	R. Cole
Grey Owl	1985	L. Rollason	Sgt Wilson	1988	R. Taylor
Grey Ridge		Les Allen	Sharman's Cross	1976	P. Ward
Helena	1959	F. Buckley	Sherwood		J. Douglas
Hetty Woolf		K. Dryden	Silverways		
Iago		D. Hadfield	Slioch		
James Arnot	1961	T. Meek	Snowy owl		L. Rollason
Lovebird		J. Douglas	Taylor's Grey		R. Taylor
Ludlow	1985	E. Pickin	Teem		T. Meek
Maggie	1966	A. Hawkes	Tenby Grey		
Magpie	1960	F. Buckley	The Brise		
Manka		J. Ballard	Trojan	1930	J. Douglas
Margaret Martin	1973	A.J. Martin	True Briton		
Mere Peppermint		Les Allen	Victoria		D. Hadfield
Nicholas Loakes			Walhampton	1961	C.G. Haysom
Oakie		D. Hadfield	Warwick	1976	P. Ward
Orlando		D. Hadfield	White Cap		D. Hadfield
Pikey		B. Taylor	White Ensign		J. Douglas
Ptarmigan		T. Coop	White Satin	2001	A. Chadwick
Queen's Bower	1967	C.G. Haysom	White Wings	1930	J. Douglas
Ray Grey	1980	R. Downard	Yorkshire Grey	1970	A. Hawkes

FANCY AURICULA CULTIVARS

This type of auricula has had its detractors in the past but now comprises some very lovely flowers. Some of the colour combinations are particularly pleasing on the eye and they look good at the shows.

Name	Year	Breeder	Colour
Alien		Tim Coop	Green/purple
Angela Short	2000	P. Redfern	Green/red
Astolat	1971	W.R. Hecker	Green/pink
Best Wishes	1988	Les Allen	Grey/pink
Blue Boy		D. Hadfield	Grey/blue
Blue Chip		D. Coop	An early-flowering grey/blue
Bold Tartan	1988	J. Radford	Red/grey
Bramshill		G. Douglas	Red/green
Brenda's Dillema		Brenda Hyatt	Red/green
Broughton	1988	G. Douglas	Red/green
Claudia Taylor		House of Douglas	Red/green
Clouded Yellow		Tim Coop	Grey/yellow
Clunie		House of Douglas	Cerise/green

Name	Year	Breeder	Colour
Coffee		G. Baker	Pale brown/grey
Colonel Champney's	1867	W. Turner	Ancient variety of maroon with a green edge
Confederate	1995	F. Taylor	Grey/yellow
Corny	1999	D. Parsons	Yellow/green
Corona			Yellow/green
Crimple		Tim Coop	Green/lavender
Crinolene		Tim Coop	Green/lavender
Daffie Green			Green/purple
Donna Clancy		G. Douglas	Red/green
Douglas Green		House of Douglas	Green/red
Dream Weaver		Tim Coop	
Eileen K.			Yellow/green
Elmer Vette			Yellow/green
Error		A. Guest	Grey/purple
Etna		Tim Coop	Grey/red
Fairy Light		C. Timpson	
Fanciful		A. Hawkes	Grey/red
Fancy Pants		Tim Coop	
Fanfare		Tim Coop	Green/red
Fleecy	1999	D. Parsons	White/pink
Fleet Street	2002	H. Pugh	Red
Florence Brown			Red
Frank Taylor		B. Hyatt	
Frosty		Tim Coop	
Gateshead		R. Beckwith	Red/grey
Glasnost		P. Lister	
Glenelg		House of Douglas	Almost black body/green edge
Golden Eye		D. Hadfield	Grey/yellow
Grace Ellen			
Green Finger			Green/yellow
Green Frills			
Green Isle		J. Douglas	Red/green
Green Meadows	1970	J. Ballard	Yellow/green
Green Mustard	2000	A. Guest	Yellow/green
Green Peace		J. Fielding	Green/yellow
Green Shank		G. Douglas	Green/red
Greenjacket			
Greta		J. Douglas	Red/grey/green
Grey Monarch	1959	J. Douglas	Yellow/grey
Grey Shrike		J. Douglas	Yellow
Hawkwood	1970	J. Douglas	Red/grey
Hawkwood Fancy		J. Douglas	Red
Hazel's Fancy		R. Barter	Yellow

Name	Year	Breeder	Colour
Helen Barter	1988	R. Barter	Purple
Helen Mary		R. Barter	Purple
Helena Brown		G. Douglas	Green/yellow
Hinton Admiral	1937	C.G. Haysom	
Hinton Field	1967	A.J. Martin	Green/yellow
Hot Lips	2002	House of Douglas	Pink/green
Idmiston		House of Douglas	Red/green
Jane	1999	J. Radford	Pink/green
Jessica			Yellow/green
Joan Butler		House of Douglas	
Karen Cordrey			Green/red
Lady Emma Monson		House of Douglas	Brown/red
Laverock Fancy	1983	G. Douglas	Red/green
Lisa Clara	1985	House of Douglas	Bright red and mid-green
Llety	1998	Les Allen	Red/green
Lowther Show		House of Douglas	Grey/red
Lucky Strike		J. Douglas	Red/green
Lynn Cooper			Yellow/green
Mary Poppins		T. Coop	Pink/green
Mary Taylor	1992	House of Douglas	Red/green
Mere Burgundy		Les Allen	Grey/red
Mere Ripple		Les Allen	Grey ripple
Merlin		P. Bowen	Yellow/green
Minley		G. Douglas	Green/magenta
Monet		T. Davies	Yellow/green
Monk		C. Timpson	Yellow/grey
Moon Fairy	2000	C. Timpson	Pink/green
Nantenan	1998	Les Allen	Yellow/green
Nigel		H. Pugh	Grey/red
No Deal		House of Douglas	Orange
Old England		House of Douglas	Red/green/grey
Ordvic/2nd Vic		Lingen Nursery	Green/yellow
Parakeet			Yellow
Pastures New	2002	T. Mitchell	Yellow/green
Patricia Barras	1985	G. Douglas	Red/green
Portree	1984	House of Douglas	Green/red
Queen Bee		H. Blackburn	Deep red with a grey edge
Rajah	1950	J. Douglas	Scarlet/green
Redstart	1962		Green/red
Rita			Green/yellow
Rolts			Red/green
Rondy		B. Wooley	Yellow
Ruddy Duck	1999	T. Meek	Red
Salad	1982	T. Meek	Yellow

Name	Year	Breeder	Colour
Showtime		Tim Coop	Grey/red
Silverfields		Tim Coop	
Silverway		J.F. Robinson	Grey/purple
Solario		Tim Coop	
Space Age		Tim Coop	
Spring Meadows	1957		Yellow/green
Star Wars		Tim Coop	
Star Wars 2		Martins Nest	Purple
Star Burst	1966	Les Allen	Grey/red
Stubb's Tartan		A. Stubbs	Green/red
Sweet Pastures	1957	J. Ballard	Yellow/grey
Tim's Fancy	1996	Tim Coop	Red
Tinker		F. Taylor	Purple/green
Toddington Green		House of Douglas	Green/red
Tosca		House of Douglas	Blood red body
Trafalgar		H. Pugh	Red
Trafalgar Square		H. Pugh	Orange
Tricia		L. Wigley	Purple
White Ensign	1950	House of Douglas	

SELF AURICULA CULTIVARS

Blue selfs

The selfs are generally not as fastidious in their growing requirements as their cousins the edges. They are often earlier to flower than the edges, displaying their wide colour range, which can look jewel-like as it is set off against the white paste. The true blue self auricula is a wish that alas will never come true. Hybridizers, try as they may, have failed in the attempt. The blue as produced by the self is described as horticultural blue, which is a blue more like a light purple, mauve or violet.

Name	Year	Breeder	Name	Year	Breeder
Atlantic	1993	P. Ward	Stella	1965	R. Newton
Audrey	2004	S. Popple	Suede Shoes		
Barbara Weinz		USA	Toolyn		S. Popple
Blue Cliff		S. Popple	Trumpet Blue		D. Telford
Blue Denim	1988	Les Allen	Watchett		Tim Coop
Blue Fire	1910	J. Douglas	Windermere		Tim Coop
Blue Jean	1972	D. Telford			
Blue Moon	1998	Les Allen			
Blue Nile	1962	R. Newton			
Blue Steel		D. Coop			
Coral Sea		P. Ward			
Cuckoo Fair		G. Dawson			
Denise		S. Popple			
Douglas Blue		House of Douglas			

Name	Year	Breeder	Name	Year	Breeder
Edward Sweeney		Jack Wemyss-Cooke			
Eventide		D. Telford			
Everest Blue	1959	H.D. Hall			
Faro		D. Telford			
Fearless		House of Douglas			
Girl Guide	1971	K. Ellerton			
Isabel	1957	R. Newton			
Jac	2004	S. Popple			
Joel	1952	C. Bach			
Laphroaigh	1998	Jack Wemyss-Cooke			

Yellow selfs

The yellow selfs consist of differing shades of the colour, from the pale 'Sheila' and 'Sherbet Lemon' through to the mid-yellow 'Lemon Ice' and the darker yellows of 'Goldie' and 'Golden Fleece'. All are real treasures. Yellow self auriculas always look fresh when displayed next to blue selfs.

Name	Year	Breeder	Name	Year	Breeder
Antoc		T. Newton	Harvest Glow		T. Newton
April Moon	1988	Tim Coop	Helen	1981	Tim Coop
Beauty of Bath		K. Gould	Lady Diana	1981	Les Allen
Bendigo		J. Douglas	Leicester Square		H. Pugh
Bilton	1970	D. Telford	Lemon Drop	1984	T. Coop
Bonanza	1997	Les Allen	Lemon Ice	1991	T. Newton
Bookham Star		J. Douglas	Lisa's Smile		D. Telford
Brasso	1976	Tim Coop	Maizie		J. Douglas
Brazil	1981	D. Telford	Melody	1936	C.G. Haysom
Brompton	1976	D. Hadfield	Moneymoon	1984	Tim Coop
Choirster	1967	A.E. James	Moon Glow	1975	D. Hadfield
Cloth of Gold			O'er The Moon	1982	T. Newton
Corntime	1988	Tim Coop	Old Gold	1920	J. Douglas
Coventry Street		H. Pugh	Party Time	1984	T. Coop
Elsinore		P. Ward	Pot of Gold	1975	Gwen Baker
Fleet Street	2004	H. Pugh	Prince Charming		G. Douglas
Gleam		J. Douglas	Rachel de Thame	2000	C. Timpson
Gold Blaze			Sharon Louise	1991	K. Bowser
Gold Crest		P. Ward	Shelia	1961	A. Hawkes
Golden Fleece		L. Kaye	Sherbet Lemon		T. Coop
Golden Girl		Tim Coop	The Baron	1982	L. Kaye
Goldenhill			Tomboy	1984	T. Coop
Goldie			Upton Belle	1974	R. Rossitter
Guinea	1971	Doctor Duthie	Yellowhammer	1978	F. Buckie

Red selfs

The red selfs auriculas are very striking indeed. The postbox hues of some look particularly vibrant when displayed next to yellow self auriculas. Red self 'Scorcher' is proving very popular and is winning on the show benches

Name	Year	Breeder	Name	Year	Breeder
A. Niblett	1962	H. Cohen	Lechistan	1976	S. Kos
Alice Haysom	1935	C. Haysom	Lindley	1976	D. Telford
Bank Error		H. Pugh	Lisa's Red		D. Telford
Branno			Leicester Square		H. Pugh
Brian's Choice			Pat	1966	J. Ballard
Cherry	1968	D. Duthie	Pride of Poland		
Cherry Pie			Red Admiral		B. Coop
Cheyanne	1971	P. Ward	Red Arrows		B. Coop
Chirichua		P. Ward	Red Beret	1980	D. Telford
Consett	1976	D. Hadfield	Red Carpet	1994	B. Coop
Cortina		D. Telford	Red Embers	1989	T. Newton
Fanny Meerbeck	1879	B. Simonite	Red Gauntlet	1966	Doctor Duthie
Favourite		T. Coop	Red Rum		D. Telford
Fennay	1999		Red Queen		H. Pugh
Geronimo	1971	P. Ward	Red Sonata		
Fleet Street	2004	H. Pugh	Ring o' Bells		T. Newton
Glazebrook			Rosemary		Doctor Duthie
Grizedale		A. Kilshaw	Royal Mail		B. Coop
Harrison Weir	1908	J. Douglas	Scorcher	1993	T. Coop
Harry O		T. Coop	Sherbet Lemon		T. Coop
Headdress	1978	D. Telford	Shere	1967	K. Gould
Kiowa	1976	P. Ward	Simply Red		T. Coop
Lady Penelope	1982		Stoney Cross		
Lady Zoé	1982		The Bishop		

Dark selfs

The dark selfs constitute a small class of self auriculas. Dark self 'Mikado', more than a hundred years old now, continues to be a dominant cultivar; 'Barbarella' is doing very well at the shows too.

Name	Year	Breeder	Name	Year	Breeder
Barbarella	1980	P. Ward	Erjon	1987	T. Newton
Black Adder		T. Coop	Gizabroon	1974	D. Telford
Black Ice			Hardley		C. J. Haysom
Black Fields	1978	D. Telford	Mamba		
Consett	1973	D. Telford	Midnight	1918	J. W. Bentley
Dakota	1974	D. Telford	Mikado	1906	W. Smith
Dark Lady	2001	K. Wharton	Neat and Tidy	1955	Dr. Newton
Douglas Black		J. Douglas	Night Dance	2002	B. Coop

Name	Year	Breeder	Name	Year	Breeder
Nightwink	1998	T. Newton	The Raven	1978	B. Simonite
Nightshift		T. Newton	The Snods	1974	D. Telford
Nocturne	1955	Dr. Newton	Wincha	1982	T. Coop
Satchmo	1978	D. Telford	Wor Jackie		D. Telford
Super Para	1974	D. Telford			

Any other colours

This class of selfs contains various colours than do not fall into the regular classes. Cultivars 'Limelight' and 'Whistle Jacket' do particularly well at the shows.

Name	Year	Breeder	Colour
Amber Light	1986	R. Rollason	Dark yellow
Annie Tustin		Jack Weymss-Cooke	Brown
Bella Zana		C. Bach	Pink
Bengal Rose		J. Kemp	Pink
Chaffinch			Pink
Chanel		Tim Coop	Pink
Chiffon		Tim Coop	Lavender/pink
Eaton Dawn		B. Coop	Pinkish
Glazenbrook			Purple
Humphrey		F. Taylor	Pinkish
Lavenham		Tim Coop	Lavender
Lepton Jubilee		J. Gibson	Lavender
Limelight		Tim Coop	Vary pale creamy green
Lookalike		D. Hadfield	Pale yellow
Marshmallow		Tim Coop	Lavender
Miss Otis		B. Coop	Pinkish
Moonlight		M. Horner	Pale yellow
Nightwick	2002	T. Newton	Dark red
Opal		B. Coop	Mushroom
Pink Gin		D. Tilt	Pinkish
Pink Lilac		J. Gibson	Pinkish
Pink Panther		J. Gibson	Pinkish
Purple Promise			Purple
Purple Sage	1970	D. Telford	Purple
Rocksand			Dark yellow
Rosanna		L. Kaye	Pinkish
Rosebud	1950	J. Douglas	Pinkish
Rosie		J. Douglas	Dark pink
Smart Tar		D. Newton	Dark blue
Star Flowers			Violet blue
Strawberry Fields	2002	Tim Coop	Pinkish
Sugar Plum Fairy		L. Rollason	Light pink

Name	Year	Breeder	Colour
Sweet Chestnut		D. Telford	Dark red
Tudor Rose	1998	S. Craverns	Medium pink
Whistle Jacket		Tim Coop	Brown
Wye Orange		F. Taylor	Orange

STRIPED AURICULA CULTIVARS

The auricula breeders D. Parsons and A. Hawkes are the dominant raisers of the back-in-fashion stripes. Cultivars 'Marian Tiger' and 'Night and Day' are currently winning at the shows.

Name	Year	Breeder	Colour
Angel Eyes	1999	D. Parsons	Purple/white
Angela Short		P. Redfern	Red/green
Anything Goes	2004	D. Parsons	Pale pink
Arundel Stripe	1986	R. Downward	Maroon/white
Blue Heaven	1999	D. Parsons	Blue/grey
Bold Tartan	1997	J. Radford	Red/green
Bollen Tiger		A. Hawkes	
Celtic One	1999	D. Parsons	Green/red
Cutie Pie	2002	D. Parsons	Orangy/green
High Hopes	1998	D. Parsons	Brown/yellow
Karen Cordrey	1988		Red/green
Kissy Kate	1999	D. Parsons	Pink/white
Königin der Nacht	1988	A. Guest	Dark violet/white
Lofty	1999	D. Parsons	Mauve/white
Lord Saye and Sele	1987	A. Hawkes	Green/orange
Marian Tiger		A.Hawkes	Red/grey
Mazetta Stripe	1988	A. Hawkes	Brown/yellow
Merlin Stripe		A. Hawkes	Green/red
Mersey Tiger			Green/red
Mrs Dargan	1800		Cream/pink
Naughty	1999	D. Parsons	Red/white
Night and Day	1999	D. Parsons	Mauve/white
Orwell Tiger	1994	A. Hawkes	Red/white
Pink Sand	2002	D. Parsons	Pink/grey
Poppet	2004	D.Parsons	Yellow/green
Purple Rose	1999	D. Parsons	Purple/grey
Raleigh Stripe	1979	A. Hawkes	Red/brown
Stardust	1999	D. Parsons	Pink/green
Three Way Stripe			Green/white/black
Wye Hen	1998		

Bibliography

BOOKS

Abercrombie, J., *The British Fruit Gardener* (Printed for Lockyer Davis, 1779).

Amstutz, Dr W., and Herdeg, W., *Alpenblumenfibel* (F. Bruckmann, Munich, 1936).

Biffen, Sir R., *The Auricula: The Story of a Florist's Flower* (Garden Book Club, London, 1951).

Bradley, R., *New Improvements of Planting and Gardening* (Printed for W. Mears, 1726).

Douglas, J., *Hardy Florists' Flowers* (London, 1880).

Emmerton, I., *Plain Treatise on the Culture of Auriculas* (Self-published, 1816).

Gerard, J., *The Herball or Generall Historie of Plantes* (London, 1597), pp.784–7.

Gilbert, S., *A Florist's Vade Mecum* (Printed for T. Simmons, 1682).

Gregg, T., *The Handbook of Fruit Culture* (unknown publisher, 1857).

Guénin, S., *Traité de la Culture Parfait de l'Orielle d'Ours ou Auricule* (Chez Henry Frikx, 1735).

Hanmer, Sir T., *The Garden Book of Sir Thomas Hanmer* (Gerard Howe, London, completed in 1659 but unpublished until 1933).

Hogg, T., *A Treatise on the Carnation and Other Flowers*, 6th edn (Whittaker and Co., 1839).

Howard Spring, Marion, *Memories and Gardens* (Collins, 1964).

Hughes, William, *The Complete Vineyard* (Printed by G.M. for W. Crooks, London, 1665).

Hughes, William, *The Flower Garden* (unknown publisher, 1671).

Johnson, G.W., *The Gardener's Monthly Volume: The Auricula Its Culture and History* (Baldwin, 1847), p.59.

Laird, M., *The Flowering of the Landscape Garden: English Pleasure Grounds 1720–1800* (University of Pennsylvania Press, 1999).

Linnaeus, C., and Clifford, G., *Hortus Cliffortianus* (originally published in Amsterdam, 1737).

Moreton, C.O., *The Auricula: Its History and Character* (Ariel Press, 1964).

Parkinson, J., *Paridisi in Sole Paradisus Terrestris* (Lownes and Young, London, 1629).

Parkinson, J., *Theatrum Botanicum* (Thomas Cotes, London, 1640).

Rea, J., *Flora: seu, De Florum Cultura or A complete Florilege Furnished With all Requisites belonging to a Florist* (unknown publisher, 1676).

Thornton, Dr R., *The Temple of Flora: Garden of Nature, with Picturesque Botanical Plates of the new Illustration of the Sexual System of Linnaeus*, 3 vols (Self-published, London, 1799–1807).

INTERNET

Dietzsch, Barbara Regina, *Auricula and Peony Bouquets*, no date, at www.georgeglazer.com/ prints/nathist/botanical/ dietzschfrmd.html (accessed January 2010).

McEwen, C., 'Music Hiding in the Air', a memoir of Rory McEwan (1932–82), no date, at www.archipelago.org/vol 4-3/mcewan.html (accessed January 2010).

Jensen, Johan Laurentz, *Pansies, Appleblossoms, Gloxinia, Phlox and Primula Auricula on a Brown Marble Ledge*, 1835, at www. artsunlight.com/artist-NJ/N-J0004/Johan Laurentz Jensen.html (accessed January 2010).

Georg Dionysius Ehret, Wikipedia entry at en.wikipedia.org/wiki/Georg_ Dionysius_Ehret (accessed January 2010).

Fine Rare Botanical Prints, no date, *Primroses Auriculas*, no date, at www.finerareprints. com (accessed January 2010).

Reinagle, Philip, *A Group of Auriculas*, no date, at www.georgeglazer.com/ prints/nathist/botanical/ PhilipReinagle (accessed January 2010).

Moon, H.G., *Auricula Mrs Moore + Prince of Greens + Charles Perry*, no date, at www.meemelink. com/flowerandfruitprints/ primulceae (accessed January 2010).

van Huysum, Jan, *Flowers in a Terracotta Vase*, 1736–7, at www.nationalgallery. org.uk/paintings/jan-van-huysum-flowers-in-a-terracotta-vase (accessed January 2010).

van Brussel, Paulus Theodorus, *Flowers in a Vase*, 1789, at www.nationalgallery.org. uk/paintings/paulus-theodorus-van-brussel-flowers-in-a-vase (accessed January 2010).

The National Auricula and Primula Society Northern Section, at www.auriculas.org.uk, 2009.

RECOMMENDED FURTHER READING

Biffen, R. Sir Roland FRS, *The Auricula* (Garden Book Club, 1951).

Marshal, Alexander, *Mr Marshal's Flower Book* (Royal Collection Enterprises Ltd, 2008).
McClain, Molly, *Beaufort the Duke and Duchess 1657–1715* (New Haven and London, Yale University Press, 2001).
Stuart, David and Sutherland, James, *Plants from the Past* (Viking, 1987).

Notes

1 Gerard, J., *The Herball or Generall Historie of Plantes* (London, 1597), pp.784–7.
2 Hanmer, Sir T., *The Garden Book of Sir Thomas Hanmer* (Gerard Howe, London, completed in 1659 but unpublished until 1933), p.80.
3 Quoted from 'Parsonage Gardens' at www.rectorysociety.org.uk (accessed January 2010).
4 Johnson, G.W., *The Gardener's Monthly Volume: The Auricula Its Culture and History* (Baldwin, 1847), p.21–2.

5 Amstutz, W., and Herdeg, W., *Alpenblumenfibel* (F. Bruckmann, Munich, 1936), p.22.
6 Abercrombie, J., Thomas, M., and other gardeners, *Every Man His Own Gardener being a new and much more complete Gardener's Kalender than any one hitherto published* (Printed for W. Griffin, London, 1767), p.132.
7 Ibid., p.132.
8 Ibid., p.133.
9 Biffen, Sir R., *The Auricula: The Story of a Florist's Flower* (Garden Book Club, London, 1951), p.38.

10 Ibid., p.39.
11 Johnson, *Gardener's Monthly Volume*, pp.59–61.
12 Ibid, p.58.
13 Ibid., pp.59–60.
14 Ibid., p.64.
15 Biffen, *The Auricula*, p.71.
16 Ibid.
17 Ibid., p.78.
18 Ibid., p.84.
19 Hogg, T., *A Practical Treatise on the Cultivation of the carnation, pink, auricula, polyanthus, ranunculus, tulip, hyacinth, rose, and other flowers* (Whittaker and Co., 1839), p.127.

Further Information

The author's own website, www.gardeningknowledge. co.uk, features pages on varied aspects of gardening, including a monthly gardening task list, clematis culture and ornamental grasses.

SOCIETIES

Auricula societies

The National Auricula and Primula Society (Northern Section)
The Honorary Secretary Mr R. Taylor
Temple Rhydding Drive
Baildon
Shipley
BD17 5PX

The National Auricula and Primula Society (Midlands and West Section)
The Honorary Secretary David Tarver
9 Church Street
Belton
Loughborough
Leicestershire
LE12 9UG

The National Auricula and Primula Society (Southern Section)
The Honorary Secretary Lawrence Wigley
67 Warnham Court Road
Carshalton Beeches
Surrey
SM5 3ND

The Ancient Society of York Florists
Secretary Mr A. Robinson
10 Jennifer Grove
York
YO24 4DZ

The American Primrose and Auricula Society (commonly referred to as The American Primrose Society)
Treasurer Jon Kawaguchi
3524 Bowman Court
Alameda
CA 94502
USA

Related societies

The Alaska Rock Garden Society
PO Box 244136
Anchorage
AK 99524-4136
USA

The Alpine Garden Society
AGS Centre, Avon Bank
Pershore
Worcestershire
WR10 3JP

The Hardy Plant Society
Little Orchard
Great Comberton
Pershore
Worcestershire
WR10 3DP

The North American Rock Garden Society
PO Box 18604
Raleigh
NC 26619-8604
USA

The Scottish Rock Garden Club
PO Box 14063
Edinburgh
EH10 4YE
Scotland

AURICULA SUPPLIERS

Abriachan Garden Nursery
Loch Ness-Side

Inverness
IV3 8LA
Scotland
Tel: 01463 861232
Email: info@lochnessgarden. com
Web: www.lochnessgarden. com

Angus Plants
3 Balfour Cottages
Menmuir by Brechin
Angus
DD9 7RW
Scotland
Tel: 01356 660280
Email: alison@angusplants. co.uk
Web: www.angusplants.co.uk

Ashwood Nurseries
Ashwood Lower Lane
Kingswinford
West Midlands
DY6 0AE
Tel: 01384 401996
Email: mailorder@ ashwoodnurseries.com
Web: www.ashwood-nurseries. co.uk

Barnhaven Primroses
11 rue du pont Blanc
22310 Plestin Les Grèves
France
Tel: +33 (0) 2 96 35 68 41
Email: info@barnhaven.com
Web: www. barnhavenprimroses.com

Cairnsmore Nursery
Chapmanton Road
Castle Douglas
DG7 2NU
Scotland
Tel: 01556 504 819
Email: info@cairnsmorenursery. co.uk
Web: www.cairnsmorenursery. co.uk

Crescent Plants
Stoney Cross
Marden
Hereford
HR1 3EW
Tel: 01432 880262
Email: june@auriculas.co.uk

Drointon Nurseries
Plaster Pitts
Norton Conyers
Ripon
North Yorkshire
HG4 5EF
Tel: 01765 641849
Email: info@auricula-plants.
co.uk
Web: www.auricula-plants.
co.uk

Farmyard Nurseries
Llandysyul
Carmarthenshire
SA44 4RL
Wales
Tel: 01559 363389
Email: richard@
farmyardnurseries.co.uk
Web: www.farmyardnurseries.
co.uk

Hillview Hardy Plants
Worfield
Nr Bridgnorth
Shropshire
WV15 5NT
Tel/Fax: +44 (0)1746 716454
Email: hillview@themutual.net
Web: www.hillviewhardyplants.
com

Les Allen
'Windy Ridge'
Llandrindod Wells
Powys
LD1 5NY
Wales
Email: leslie.allen@
mypostoffice.co.uk
(National collection holder)

Peninsula Plants
72 Ballyeasborough Road
Kircubbin
County Down
BT 22 1AD
Northern Ireland
Tel: 028 4277 2193
Email: Peninsula.primulas@
btinternet.com
Web: www.
primulasandauriculas.com

Pop's Plants
Pop's Cottage, Barford Lane
Downton
Salisbury
Wiltshire
SP5 3PZ
Tel: 01725 511421
Email: mail@popsplants.com
Web: www.popsplants.com
(National Collection Holder)

Timpany Nurseries and Garden
Magheratimpany Road
Ballynahinch
County Down
BT24 8PA
Northern Ireland
Email: s.tindall@btconnect.com

Glossary

anther The tip of the stamen; it contains the pollen.

body colour The main colour of the petal on the edge and fancy auricula types.

calyx The sepals in a cup shape that protect the bud when it is expanding.

carrot The expanded top portion of the root (the rhizome).

centre The centre part of the petal of white through to yellow on alpine auriculas.

corolla The collective term for the petals.

cultivar A cultivated variety.

edge The show varieties that have an outer petal edge of green, white or grey.

eye The white disc covered in farina.

farina *syn.* meal: The white powdery coating of leaves, stems and flowers on some auriculas, also called the paste.

footstalk *syn.* pedicel: The stem or stalk holding an individual flower (pip).

gouache A method of painting that uses opaque pigments, ground in water and thickened with glue.

ground colour The ring of colour of an edged auricula; the body colour.

meal *See* farina *and* paste.

ovary The lower part of the pistil that bears the ovules.

paste The circle of dense farina (also called the meal) at the centre of show auriculas.

pedicel *syn.* footstalk: The stem or stalk holding an individual flower (pip).

peduncle The stalk or main stem of a flower truss.

petal The individual showy coloured part of a flower.

petiole The leaf stalk.

pin The stigma.

pin-eyed When the stigma and style are growing above the stamen. Plants can thus be disqualified from shows, apart from the border types.

pip The individual flower as part of the truss.

pistil The collective part of the female reproductive organs: stigma, style and ovary.

pollen The powdery substance emitted by the anthers to fertilize the pistil.

rhizome The thickened part of the root, also called the carrot, from where roots and shoots emanate.

scape The leafless flower stalk (stem) that grows from the centre of the plant to carry the flowers.

stamen The collective part of the male reproductive organs: the anther and filament.

stigma The uppermost part of the female reproductive parts of the flowers, this receives the pollen from the anther.

style The hollow cylinder between the stigma and the ovary that transports the pollen down to the ovary.

systemic The effect of an insecticide that travels to all parts of a plant for an effective kill, or in the case of a fungicide to protect against fungal infection, also called translocated.

transpiration The loss of water through a plant's leaf (evaporation).

thrum-eyed The term given when the stamen is above the stigma at the mouth of the flower.

truss The flower head that radiates from the top of the scape.

tube The cylindrical centre of the flower that houses the collective reproductive parts.

variety A subspecies of plant; *see also* cultivar.

Index

Other Gardening Books from Crowood

Blackburne-Maze, Peter *The Complete Guide to Fruit Growing*
Blackburne-Maze, Peter *The Complete Guide to Vegetable Growing*
Clark, Emma *The Art of the Islamic Garden*
Cooke, Ian *Designing Small Gardens*
Cooke, Ian *Exotic Gardening*
Cox, Freda *Garden Styles*
Cunningham, Sally *Ecological Gardening*
Ford, Richard *Hostas – an essential guide*
Gooch, Ruth and Jonathan *Clematis – an essential guide*
Gray, Linda *Herb Gardening*
Gregson, Sally *Ornamental Vegetable Gardening*
Gregson, Sally *Practical Propagation*
Hart, Simon *Tomatoes – a gardener's guide*
Hodge, Geoff *Pruning*
Jones, Peter *Gardening on Clay*
Larter, Jack *Tuberous Begonias*
Lavelle, Michael *Sustainable Gardening*
Littlewood, Michael *The Organic Gardener's Handbook*
Marder, John *Water-Efficient Gardening*
Nottridge, Rhoda *Wildlife Gardening*
Parsons, Roger *Sweet Peas – an essential guide*
Saunders, Bridgette *Allotment Gardening*